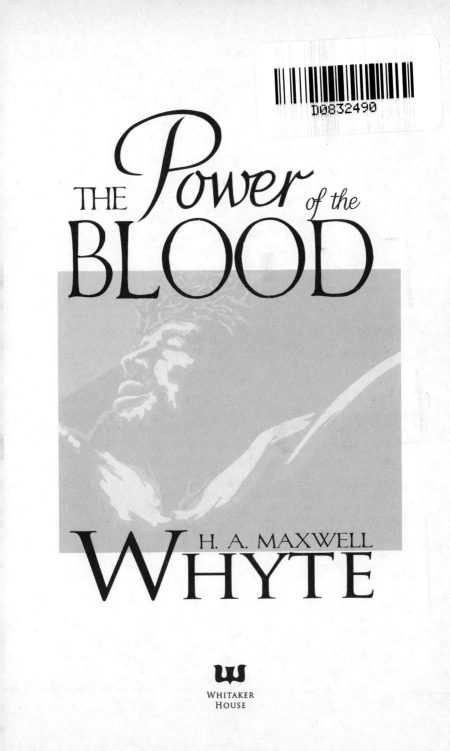

THE *Power* of the
BLOOD

H. A. MAXWELL
WHYTE

WHITAKER
HOUSE

THE POWER OF THE BLOOD

ISBN: 978-0-88368-439-9 • eBook ISBN: 978-1-60374-203-0
Printed in the United States of America
© 1973, 2005 by Whitaker House

Whitaker House
1030 Hunt Valley Circle
New Kensington, PA 15068
www.whitakerhouse.com

Library of Congress Cataloging-in-Publication Data

Whyte, H. A. Maxwell.
  The power of the blood / H. A. Maxwell Whyte.— Rev. and expanded ed.
     p. cm.
  Summary: "Examines the biblical foundations of the shed blood of Jesus Christ, as well as its potential impact in the lives of today's Christians"— Provided by publisher.
  ISBN-13: 978-0-88368-439-9 (trade pbk. : alk. paper)
  ISBN-10: 0-88368-439-X (trade pbk. : alk. paper)   1. Jesus Christ—Blood.
I. Title.
  BT590.B5W45 2005
  232'.4—dc22
                        2005012956

9 10 11 12 13 14 15 16 17 **uu** 24 23 22 21 20 19 18 17

Foreword

BY STANLEY H. FRODSHAM

It has been a great joy to read this book, and a delight to accede to the request of the author that I write a foreword.

Every fresh outpouring of the Spirit of God begins with a praying group, or with praying groups. There were two such groups in the British Isles in 1907—doubtless more, but the writer knows of these two. One group of five women met every Saturday in a small home in London to pray for an outpouring of the Spirit; the other group of five men met each Saturday night in the Episcopal rectory in Sunderland, England. The cry of both groups was for a Pentecostal outpouring in the British Isles.

The Lord came to the London group first. Catherine Price, a humble housewife, was preparing her dinner when she was constrained by the Spirit to leave everything and go to wait upon the

Lord. As she waited, Jesus came to her in person. As she magnified and glorified Him, her English was taken away and she began to praise Him in a new language.

A few days later she was led to go to a meeting in London, organized by the Keswick group, a people who stood for the highest spiritual life in those days. The service began with a song, but there seemed to be no heart in the worship. The Spirit of the Lord fell upon Catherine Price, a very timid woman, and she cried out, "Oh, how can you sing so listlessly, so apathetically, so carelessly about the blood of Jesus Christ!" Immediately she began to speak in another tongue as the Spirit gave utterance.

The effect upon the audience was tremendous. Some fell upon their faces before God; others rushed out of the building in fear. A number were deeply impressed that this was truly a manifestation of the Spirit of God, and they inquired for the address of this woman. From that day there came to her home many who desired to know more about this, and they were baptized in the Spirit. Her home was opened for meetings in which the one theme was *"Behold the Lamb of God"* (John 1:29, 36), for by the outpoured blood of the Lamb, the gift of the Holy Spirit was purchased. And so the outpouring of the Spirit began in London.

Soon the Spirit was outpoured in Sunderland; and there, as in London, the blood of Jesus Christ was extolled. As they reverently pleaded the blood of Jesus, many were filled with the Holy Spirit.

Incidentally, there was another group praying in Valparaiso, Chile, South America, in a Methodist church; the Lord poured out His Spirit upon Dr. Hoover and his Methodist brethren—a group of five who met every day for prayer. The theme of that revival was also the blood of Jesus Christ.

They greatly honored the blood in those days and constantly sang,

> Under the blood, the precious blood;
> Under the cleansing, healing blood;
> Keep me, Savior, from day to day,
> Under the precious blood.

It seemed that there was no end to the revelations of the power and the preciousness of the blood of Jesus Christ.

Now, once again, the Lord is bringing the power of the blood to the attention of the church. Let us honor and plead the blood of the Lamb very reverently, for through the blood we have power over all the might of the enemy. To those who plead the blood of the Lamb—not mechanically, but in true holy reverence—there will be a restoration of all that the locust, the cankerworm, the caterpillar, and the palmerworm have eaten (Joel 2:25).

—*Stanley H. Frodsham*
Ontario, Canada
August 1959

Preface to the Newly Revised and Expanded Edition

Besides his worldwide preaching and deliverance ministry, H. A. Maxwell Whyte wrote many books on related topics. Most of these were produced at minimal cost for distribution to those who desired a deeper understanding and appreciation of healing and deliverance. Only a few of his works have been published and widely distributed. The best known is *The Power of the Blood,* which has sold well over 500,000 copies worldwide in its earlier editions in several languages.

In his preface to the mass-market edition, Whyte stated, "Everywhere it has been my privilege to minister, the message on the blood has been received with gladness, and many have thereby been healed and filled with the Holy Spirit. On every hand it seems that God has again revealed to Christians that they should 'plead the precious blood of Jesus.'"

In addition to *The Power of the Blood,* Whyte authored a wealth of insightful material on the tenets of the charismatic movement. Perhaps the most prevalent theme throughout his works is the power of the blood of Jesus Christ. This newly revised and expanded edition is a compilation of Whyte's rich writings on the subject of the blood, gleaned from material he authored during the last twenty years of his ministry. It is powerful and uplifting, describing and explaining his experiences and beliefs about the wonderful gifts of the Spirit and the precious blood of Jesus. He presents his thoughts in a compelling and dynamic way, guided by the Holy Spirit. The original text is included in its entirety, along with excerpts from the following, which are some of Whyte's other writings:

Bible Baptisms
Charismatic Gifts
Demons and Deliverance
Divine Health
How to Receive the Baptism in the Holy Spirit
Is Mark 16 True?
Pulling Down Strongholds

As it is covered in this new edition, Whyte's entire body of thought on the precious blood of the Lamb will add depth to our understanding of this most vital, yet seldom wielded, weapon in the believer's arsenal. We pray that Pastor Whyte's lifetime of prayer, study, and teaching will live on in the hearts and minds of many thousands of believers.

—*The Publisher*
May 2005

Contents

Foreword by Stanley H. Frodsham 3

Preface to the Newly Revised Edition 7

"There Is a Fountain Filled with Blood" 12

Chapter 1: Life Is in the Blood 15

Chapter 2: Atonement by the Blood 29

Chapter 3: The Blood Speaks 43

Chapter 4: The Passover 51

Chapter 5: The Scarlet Thread 65

Chapter 6: The Value of the Blood 83

"Arise, My Soul, Arise" 95

Chapter 7: How to Plead the Blood 97

Chapter 8: The Blood and Divine Health 109

Chapter 9: The Application of the Blood 119

Chapter 10: Holy Spirit Baptism
and the Blood 131

Chapter 11: Protection through the Blood 149

"There Is Power in the Blood" 160

Chapter 12: The New Birth and the Blood 161

Chapter 13: Wonder-Working Power
of the Blood 171

End Notes 187

About the Author 188

"There Is a Fountain Filled with Blood"
Lyrics by William Cowper, 1772

Verse 1

There is a fountain filled with blood
Drawn from Immanuel's veins;
And sinners, plunged beneath that flood,
Lose all their guilty stains.
Lose all their guilty stains, lose all their guilty stains.
And sinners, plunged beneath that flood,
Lose all their guilty stains.

Verse 2

The dying thief rejoiced to see
That fountain in his day;
And there have I, though vile as he,
Washed all my sins away.
Washed all my sins away, washed all my sins away;
And there have I, though vile as he,
Washed all my sins away.

Verse 3

Dear dying Lamb, Thy precious blood
Shall never lose its power,
Till all the ransomed church of God
Be saved, to sin no more.
Be saved, to sin no more, be saved, to sin no more.
Till all the ransomed church of God
Be saved, to sin no more.

Verse 4

E'er since by faith I saw the stream
Thy flowing wounds supply.
Redeeming love has been my theme,
And shall be till I die.
And shall be till I die, and shall be till I die.
Redeeming love has been my theme,
And shall be till I die.

one

Life Is in the Blood

"Pastor Whyte, will you pray for my eyes?" Betty asked me one day. She was a young girl of sixteen who worked in a Fish 'n' Chips store in Toronto.

"Why, certainly, Betty," I replied. "Let's just believe God together and plead the blood of Jesus." I looked at her for a moment and felt the great compassion of Jesus stirring within me. She was totally blind in her right eye, and her left eye was wandering so that it was very difficult for her to focus at all. She was wearing very, very thick glasses—the thickest she could get.

I began to pray for her, pleading the blood strongly and emphatically. Instantly, the Lord restored the sight of her right eye.

"Oh, praise the Lord!" she exclaimed. "I can see!" We rejoiced together at the mercy of the Lord.

Over a period of weeks, the wandering eye began to focus, and in a matter of months, she had twenty-twenty vision. That was twenty years ago, and she is still healed.

A MYSTERIOUS SUBSTANCE

This is but one example of hundreds upon hundreds of stories that I could relate to you that demonstrate the power of the blood of Jesus. Each story is thrilling and convincing. But first, let me share with you some of the basic teachings of the Bible about the blood.

Blood is a strange and mysterious substance. A young lad can gaze into a slaughterhouse and watch the animals' blood running down the drain without flinching; but the same boy, when grown older and with a bit more imagination, may pass out in a dead faint at the sight of blood.

On the other hand, excited men and women may clap and cheer when their favorite boxer causes blood to flow in a boxing match. It seems that the baser side of man likes to see blood; it excites him. But the nobler side of man is repulsed by blood, and sympathy is expressed at the suffering of those whose blood has been shed in accidents and war. Yes, blood is a mysterious substance.

In the Scriptures we begin to get some understanding of this amazing substance. While the Bible does not tell us about the chemical composition of the red and white corpuscles, it does tell us something that is absolutely basic to the mystery: The life of a living creature is in its blood. Thus, in Leviticus 17:11 we read, *"For the life of the flesh is in the blood."*

But *life* is as mysterious as blood, and very little is understood about it. We do know that man cannot create or copy life, even though he tries to do so in laboratories. The well-known story of Frankenstein and his monster claims to portray how life came from an electrical charge into a corpse made of human tissue; but, of course, this is pure fiction.

Life is as mysterious as blood.

It is best that we accept the fundamental truth that both electricity and life come from the Author of all life, God Almighty.

In the second chapter of Genesis, we read how God created man. It is important that we understand that man can never create man. Man is God's greatest creative achievement on earth and was made in His likeness. The Bible teaches that man is *"fearfully and wonderfully made"* (Psalm 139:14), far more wonderfully made than the angels—at least with respect to the idea that angels have no flesh or blood since they were created strictly as spirit beings. This is the way God made angels, in contrast to the way He created man.

BLOOD, THE CARRIER OF LIFE

When God made man, He formed a body from the dust of the ground, from the substances and chemicals of this planet. Then He breathed into this body the breath of life. In other words, He breathed into this composition of inert chemicals some of His own spiritual life, and that life was held in the complex substance we call blood. *"For the life of the flesh is **in** the blood"* (Leviticus 17:11, emphasis added).

So, you see, blood is not life, but it *carries* life. This becomes quite clear by observing what happens at death. Immediately after expiration, the person's body is still warm and will remain so for a brief time. Yet that person is dead because life has mysteriously departed from the blood. The life of man is carried in his bloodstream. Life itself is spiritual, but it must have a physical carrier, and this carrier is the blood.

To me, the most amazing thing about blood is its capacity to carry the gift of life that comes from God. The point of contact between the Divine and the human rests in the bloodstream. No wonder we say that blood is a mysterious substance! It contains something that no scientist can explain—it contains precious, God-given life.

In the not too distant past, it became possible to draw blood from a person's veins, seal it in special containers, and store it in newly created blood banks, where the life that alone comes from God could be kept in refrigerators much below the normal temperature of blood in a human body. Blood can even be frozen, but the life that is in it is unaffected by this freezing process.

Apart from the compatibility factor of the various blood types, it doesn't matter if the blood of a woman is given to a man, if the blood of a black donor is put into the veins of a white person, or if a skid-row bum receives a transfusion from a wealthy person. Blood does not determine the sex, the color of the skin, or the culture of the person; it simply carries the life that comes from God. There would be no chemical difference between dead blood and live blood of the same type, apart from the life that God put in it and took away from it.

Blood is the physical carrier of life.

It is possible for a person who has been seriously wounded to literally bleed to death as the heart pumps the life-giving blood out of the wound. As soon as the blood has gone, the life has gone, for the life is in the blood! One can fill the veins with chemicals, dress up the corpse, and lay it in a casket for all to see—but the corpse is still a corpse, for there is no blood in the veins and thus no life in the body.

THE UNIQUENESS OF JESUS' BLOOD

This discussion quite naturally leads to some consideration of the unique nature of Jesus' blood. I am deeply grateful to Dr. William Standish Reed of the Christian Medical Foundation of Tampa, Florida, for his thoughts on the matter of the supernatural conception of Jesus in the womb of Mary. The female ovum itself has no blood in it, and neither has the male sperm; but it is when these come together in the fallopian tube that conception takes place and a new life begins. The genetic codes in the blood cells of this new creation are inherited from both father and mother, and the blood type is determined by the combination of genetic material from both the egg and the sperm at the moment of conception. The unborn baby is thereafter protected by the placenta from any flow of the mother's blood into the fetus.

The Bible is explicit that the Holy Spirit was the Divine Agent who caused Jesus' conception in the womb of Mary. This, therefore, was not a normal conception but a supernatural act of God in planting the life of His already existent Son right in the womb of Mary, with no normal union of a male sperm with a female ovum from Mary. As the blood of the Son of God was of an entirely separate and precious nature, it is inconceivable that Mary could have supplied any of her Adamic, unregenerate blood for the spotless Lamb of God. All the Child's blood came from His Father in heaven by a supernatural creative act of God. Jesus' blood was without the Adamic stain of sin.

The idea held by many that Mary supplied the ovum and that the Holy Spirit supplied the spiritual sperm would mean that Jesus would have been conceived with mixed blood, part of Adam and part of God, which is repugnant to God's plan of salvation for a fallen human race. Such an erroneous idea

The blood of Jesus has its own unique, precious nature.

also lends encouragement to the view held by some in the metaphysical cults that Jesus had no existence prior to His conception in the womb of Mary.

The fact of the matter is that God says in the Bible that He prepared a body for His Son. *"Wherefore when he cometh into the world, he saith, Sacrifice and offering thou wouldest not, but a body thou hast prepared for me"* (Hebrews 10:5). It was *that* body that was implanted in Mary's womb. Jesus knew before His birth at Bethlehem that His Father would build and prepare a body for Him, which He later described as the temple of God (John 2:21). He simply came down from heaven and entered into the newly created body in the womb of Mary, His earthly mother. This body had blood created by His Father. There was no Adamic intermixing.

Jesus was *"the only begotten of the Father"* (John 1:14), and His body was formed and fashioned wonderfully in the womb of Mary, His mother. But the life that was in Jesus Christ came uniquely from the Father by the Holy Spirit. Therefore, this life that flowed in the veins of the Lord Jesus Christ came from God alone. No wonder He said, *"I am…the life"* (John 14:6). God imparted His own life into the bloodstream of Jesus. Adamic blood is corrupt and was carried by Mary, who declared that Jesus her Son was *"God my Saviour"* (Luke 1:47). Mary was the chosen carrier of the body of her Son, but all of His blood came from God.

BLOOD TYPES, PURE AND TAINTED

A limited number of categories or types of human blood have been catalogued by medical science (A+, B+, AB+, O+, O-, AB-, B-, and A-), but I am certain that the blood "type" of the Lord Jesus Christ was entirely different. The blood that flowed in His veins was perfect since it was not contaminated by Adam's sin, which brought sin and sickness into human blood.

If Adam had not sinned, he would not have died. But by his sin, he introduced death into the human family. The human body, therefore, became subject to corruption and decay, and death ultimately comes to each one of us. It is at the moment of death that the life in the blood takes its departure from the physical body, along with the spirit and soul of man.

Jesus Christ had no sin in His body, but He allowed Himself to die for the sins of a sinful humanity. He gave the perfect life that was in His perfect blood to redeem imperfect mankind— whose bodies carry death because of sin—in an exchange of pure blood for contaminated blood, life for death, *"for the life...is in the blood."* This is why Jesus is described as the last Adam. God sent Him to earth in the *likeness* of sinful Adam, but with pure, uncontaminated blood in His veins. God sent Him so that He might shed that pure blood of His for the life of humanity.

It is very important for us to understand that the blood of Jesus is in a completely different category from ours. Peter rightly described it as *"precious blood"* (1 Peter 1:19). It is not possible to assess the value of Jesus' blood in human terms.

It is priceless. It is God's price for the redemption of the whole human race.

SPIRITUAL TRANSFUSIONS

Stretch your imagination for a moment. Wouldn't it be wonderful if Jesus' blood could be kept in the blood banks of our hospitals? Don't you see that everyone who could obtain a transfusion of Christ's blood would actually be receiving God's eternal life in pure blood? Of course, God never meant to administer salvation by blood transfusions! But a miracle just as great takes place when a man trusts in Jesus and accepts Him as his personal Savior. Immediately, a great cleansing takes place, and the sin that is in the bloodstream is purged. *For I will cleanse their blood that I have not cleansed: for the LORD dwelleth in Zion"* (Joel 3:21).

When we receive Jesus, the Bible expresses the idea that the *heart* is cleansed by the blood of Jesus. (See, for example, 2 Chronicles 30:18–19; Hebrews 9:14; 1 John 1:7.) This may be more literal than some would dare to believe. If the sin and corruption in our bloodstream is purged and all spiritual filth is washed out, then certainly the very heart that pumps the blood may be spoken of as being cleansed. By the miracle of salvation, we receive both eternal life and the divine health of the Son of God. The greatest disinfectant in the world is the blood of Jesus Christ. It carries the eternal life of God in it.

DEAD BLOOD, LIVE BLOOD

In this connection it is interesting to note that Satan's nickname *Beelzebub* means "lord of the flies," or "prince of the flies." Dead blood will quickly attract flies, which will breed corruption in the coagulating blood. However, the blood of Jesus has exactly the opposite effect: It repulses Beelzebub and all his demons. When you put the blood of Jesus on something by faith, Satan will flee because the blood of Jesus is alive. The life is in the blood.

The devil hates the mention of the blood of Jesus. This is very evident in our deliverance ministry when demons talk to us. I have heard some demons actually wail, "Don't say that; don't say that," when we mentioned the blood of Jesus. Another demon said accusingly, "You said that!" as though we had said some terrible thing.

One time we were praying for a woman who was insane. "Jesus," I said, "we plead Your precious blood!" Immediately, a strange voice came out of the woman's throat. "Don't say that," the voice growled. "I don't like that!"

But we persisted. "We plead the blood!" we cried. Finally the demon gave up. "All right, you can say it—I don't mind," it said. "Anyway, it's all dried up; it's all dried up!" With that, the demon went out, and the woman was restored to sanity. Again we rejoiced at the power of the blood.

DELIVERANCE TO LIFE

A beautiful sixteen-year-old girl once approached me for prayer. She seemed the type you would meet at church, but Satan is an arch deceiver. This girl first told me that she had been on drugs. Then she confessed that she had also been acting as a witch at school. Apparently she had two demons.

I laid my hands upon her head, rebuked the demons, and commanded them to come out in Jesus' name.

Immediately they started to scream, for they realized their helplessness before the name of Jesus and His shed blood. They screamed and choked her for nearly an hour. Many surprised Christian students began to intercede for her until she was completely delivered.

I asked her if she would like to be filled with the Holy Spirit. She readily agreed, and she was taught to plead and honor the blood of Jesus in prayer. Soon the Holy Spirit entered into her, and she began to speak in a beautiful unknown tongue! I marveled at the wonderful change that Jesus brought to her countenance.[1]

Never underestimate the power of the blood of Jesus. In Leviticus, we read,

> *For the life of the flesh is in the blood: and I have given it to you upon the altar to make an atonement for your souls: for it is the blood that maketh an atonement for the soul.* (Leviticus 17:11)

The author of Hebrews, therefore, made no mistake when he wrote, *"Without shedding of blood is no remission"* (Hebrews 9:22).

two

Atonement by the Blood

Imagine, if you can, the scene at Calvary. No artist has ever pictured the crucifixion as it really was. It would be too repulsive to paint on any canvas. It is doubtful that the Romans left Jesus even the courtesy of a loincloth. He became as exposed as the first Adam in the garden so that He might cover His own nakedness—and thus our exposed sins, which He had taken upon Himself—with His own precious blood.

In turn, we may cover our spiritual nakedness with His precious blood—a perfect atonement or covering indeed! We cannot even offer a convenient loincloth or fig leaf to hide our sins; we must divest ourselves of everything and appear destitute of all covering in His presence. Then He will give us His own blessed robe of righteousness after we have accepted the cleansing of His precious blood. A glorious truth indeed!

THE ULTIMATE BLOOD SACRIFICE

The crown of thorns was put upon His head, not gently but roughly. Many thorns—perhaps a dozen or more—up to one-and-a-half inches long, were jabbed into His scalp, producing such serious wounds that trickles of blood spurted out and ran into His hair and beard, matting both in dark red. The spikes were driven into the wrists of His hands, and His blood coursed down His arms and sides. Spikes were also driven through His feet, and more blood ran down the sides of the cross on behalf of the sins of the whole world. Later a spear was thrust into His side, and His blood spilled out (John 19:34) and ran down the cross onto the ground beneath.

Atonement was provided by Christ's blood sacrifice.

His bones were out of joint (Psalm 22:14). His face was dreadful to look at, His features unrecognizable. (See Isaiah 53.) Since He was already dead when the soldiers arrived to break His legs—which was their custom in order to hasten death—not a bone of Him was broken (Psalm 34:20; John 19:36). Those who looked on Him saw only blood. It was a spectacle of blood. His hair and beard were soaked in His own blood. His back was lacerated from the thirty-nine stripes and was covered with His own blood. The cross was soaked with blood, as well as the ground around the base of the cross. It was blood, blood, blood everywhere.

It is important for us to grasp the fact that complete atonement is provided for us through the blood of Christ. The word *atonement* is a beautiful word, which is unfortunately sometimes misunderstood. One group has offered the suggestion that the word *atonement* means "at-one-ment." The best we can say for this is that it is an apt play on words, but not the literal meaning. The word *atonement* simply means "a covering." *"Where sin abounded, grace did much more abound"* (Romans 5:20), for with grace came the blood of Jesus, which, freely given in love, covers all our sins. (See Proverbs 10:12; Romans 4:7; 1 Peter 4:8.)

THE FAMILY BOMB SHELTER

The effectiveness of the covering by the blood of Jesus was made very real to Mrs. Whyte and me during World War II when we were living in England. We often experienced dangerous air raids, during which buzz bombs were flying everywhere. But we were able to lie down with our children and sleep through much of the peril.

The protection afforded by the blood of Jesus was so real that it seemed as if we were sleeping in a strong shelter. In fact, we used to speak of the blood as the "best air-raid shelter in the world." However, we never took this shelter for granted. Instead, every night before we went to sleep, we would cover ourselves, our home, and our children with the blood of Jesus. One night thirteen bombs landed within a three-quarter-mile radius of our home. And they were big blockbusters. Yet aside from some minor damage to the house, we were all kept safe.

GOD'S LOVE COVERS OUR SINS

If we can clearly understand the meaning of the word *atonement*, we have discovered tremendous truth. God has provided a substance by which we can cover things we no longer want; God guarantees not even to see our sins after we reckon by faith that the blood of Jesus has covered them. Why is this? Because when God sees the blood of the Lamb, He does not see sin.

We are told in Leviticus that not only is the life in the blood, but the blood is also the only substance that can make an atonement, or covering, for our souls.

> *For the life of the flesh is in the blood: and I have given it to you upon the altar to make an atonement for your souls: for it is the blood that maketh an atonement for the soul.* (Leviticus 17:11)

The sinner, upon accepting a substitute—in Old Testament times, it was a clean animal, but since the crucifixion, it is Jesus Himself—sees the substitute dying in his place. In this way, a blood covering was and is provided for the sinner.

"FIG-LEAF" RELIGIONS

At the beginning of creation, God commanded that living creatures, greatly beloved of Adam, must be slaughtered and their blood must be shed to supply a covering for Adam and Eve's obvious nakedness. Fig leaves were insufficient. So animals were slaughtered, and after the blood was shed, Adam and Eve were covered with the skins. The principle of a life for a life runs throughout the Bible. No other garments would sufficiently cover Adam and Eve except those that involved the shedding of blood. If man is left to himself, he usually invents a religion that does not require the shedding of blood—a "fig-leaf" religion.

This is why it is exceedingly important that, in observing the Lord's Supper, we partake of both the bread and the wine. To take of the bread only, as some groups do, would be equivalent to a bloodless offering, for there is no life in the flesh without blood.

IN PERFECT HARMONY

In 1 John 5:8, we read, *"And there are three that bear witness in earth, the Spirit, and the water, and the blood: and these three agree in one."* In the

Scriptures, water is often a symbol of the Word of God; it is what washes us continually, as we see in Ephesians 5:26. But the Word without the blood is ineffectual, for the life of Jesus, who is the Word of God, is in the blood. Therefore, in the Lord's Supper, it is not proper to receive the bread alone. We are to receive both bread and wine, which speaks of Jesus, the crucified Word of God, and the blood that He willingly shed.

The Holy Spirit is also in complete agreement with the water and the blood. For this reason, when we honor the blood of Jesus, the Holy Spirit immediately manifests His life on our behalf. The Holy Spirit agrees with the Word of God and with the blood of Jesus, and all three are in agreement with the others. They are triunely one.

GOD'S EQUATIONS

For there are three that bear record in heaven, the Father, the Word, and the Holy Ghost: and these three are one. And there are three that bear witness in earth, the Spirit, and the water, and the blood: and these three agree in one.

(1 John 5:7–8)

There is a most wonderful equation in 1 John 5:7–8. In fact there are two equations, one dealing with God's operations in heaven and the second with His workings on earth.

Equation # 1: Operations in Heaven

Three that bear record in heaven =
the Father + the Word + the Holy Ghost

Now it isn't difficult for us to understand this. The Father is over all, the Son (the Word) sits on His right hand, and the Holy Spirit agrees with all that is done and is the One who visits earth continually to bless God's creation. The Holy Spirit is omnipresent in earth and heaven at the same time. There is complete agreement among the three persons of the Trinity.

Equation # 2: Workings in Earth

Three that bear witness in earth =
the Spirit + the water + the blood

This is a most remarkable triad. Notice that, where the Father was first in heaven, now He is replaced on earth by the Holy Spirit, who becomes the primary focus, and the One with whom we all must deal. In heaven, the second place was given to the second person of the Trinity, Jesus, described as the Logos or the Word of God (John 1:1). The Word in heaven becomes the water on earth in the second position, because water is the symbol of the Holy Spirit and water flows. I refer you again to the words of Jesus, who said, *"Out of his belly shall flow rivers of living water"* (John 7:38). The water of the Word in heaven flows down to earth by the Holy Spirit as living water from the river of God. When this water comes into us, it must flow out of us, for we are simply to be channels, just as the vessels of the Old Testament sanctuary were for pouring out blessings, not just for containing blessings.

The Living Word, therefore, must flow, and it begins in heaven and is poured out of our mouths in the form of the living, flowing Word of God. Speaking in tongues is always God's Word flowing, and this may come forth, according to our faith, as tongues, interpretation of tongues, or prophecy, but it is always the Logos Word flowing to people to bring them refreshment and blessing.

We are channels for the Living Word to flow through.

A Christian who claims to be filled with the Spirit and who does not pour forth the Word of God supernaturally is not measuring up to the record of the Bible that the Spirit and the water agree perfectly. A Christian who does not pour forth is a dry one—his vessel has dried up. He is saved but not doing what he is supposed to do—to witness in the power of the Spirit. He is without power (Gr., *dunamis*), for Jesus said we would have His *"dunamis"* when the Holy Spirit comes upon us in Pentecostal fashion (Acts 1:8).

Notice that both the Holy Spirit and the flowing Word agree absolutely in their witness with the blood of Jesus. How can this be? The blood is living blood. It is on the mercy seat in heaven, sprinkled by the hand of Jesus when He ascended (see Hebrews 9), because in the typology in the Old Testament the High Priest sprinkled the blood of the sacrifice once a year on the gold-covered mercy seat of the ark behind the veil of the temple. The mercy seat means the place of propitiation, or mercy, where God meets with us on the common ground of the shed blood of the Lamb.[2]

BLOOD OF SPRINKLING

As recounted by the author of Hebrews, on the Day of Atonement in the Old Testament, Moses *"took the blood…and sprinkled both the book, and all the people"* (Hebrews 9:19). Why? Because the book is a lifeless book to the reader unless the blood is first applied. Both the book (the Word of God) and the people were sprinkled with the blood. This too was fulfilled on Calvary. Jesus, who is the living Word of God, was sprinkled with His own blood.

There are some who tell us that it is enough that we have the name of Jesus, but I beg to differ. We need the name *and* the blood, for the life is in the blood. There is power in the name of Jesus only because He shed His own blood and offered it to His Father, who then gave His power and His authority to His Son (Matthew 28:18). That same power and authority is given to all believers (Luke 10:19), but it becomes operative only as we honor His blood.

IN OUR PLACE

The death of Christ is often spoken of as being substitutionary. Jesus died in our place for us. Referring to the Old Testament will give abundant evidence that sins could be forgiven by God only on the grounds of shed blood—a life for a life—and we are informed of this fact in the New Testament as well: *"Without shedding of blood is no remission"* (Hebrews 9:22).

When Jesus died upon the cross, He, as God's High Priest, shed and sprinkled His own blood on behalf of the people. He was crucified at the time of the Feast of the Passover, the feast the Jews kept to remember the time when God said, "When I see the blood, I will pass over you and will not allow the destroyer to attack you." (See Exodus 12:23.) At the very time when the Jews were celebrating the first exodus, Jesus was making atonement for the second exodus. To all who will believe in His sacrifice and the efficacy of His precious blood, there is an exodus from sin and the penalty of sin, which includes sickness.

FORESHADOWING FULFILLED IN CHRIST

Every type and symbol of the atonement in the Old Testament was fulfilled in Christ. When Jesus' shed blood splattered over His body, His garments, the cross, and the ground, the following events that foreshadowed His atoning work were completed:

1. blood sprinkled on the altar (Exodus 24:6–8);
2. all around on the altar (Exodus 29:12, 16; Leviticus 7:2);
3. on the high priest and his garments (Exodus 29:20–21);
4. at the base of the altar (Leviticus 4:7);
5. on the side of the altar (Leviticus 5:9);
6. before the tabernacle seven times (Numbers 19:4).

This last was fulfilled in that the cross and the hill of Calvary were within sight of the temple in Jerusalem, for Calvary was outside the city wall.

All these Old Testament types were fulfilled in the crucifixion of Jesus, who made Himself our Passover, our High Priest, our Savior, and our blood sacrifice. His blood alone covers our sins.

JESUS BORE OUR GUILT

When we consider the great load of sin and guilt that Jesus carried on Calvary, is it any wonder that He cried out in agony, not so much of body, but of soul, *"My God, my God, why hast thou forsaken me?"* (Psalm 22:1; Matthew 27:46). But why had the Father forsaken the Son? Because it is written that God cannot look upon sin (Habakkuk 1:13). When Jesus was bearing the sins of the world in His body on the cross, the Father could not look at His Son. Jesus had become sin for us (2 Corinthians 5:21).

Since Jesus was bearing the guilt of *"our sins in his own body"* (1 Peter 2:24), it was not possible for the Father to look upon Him until Jesus had covered His own body with His blood and died. Only then could the Father turn and gaze again upon His only begotten Son. He had been *"obedient unto death, even the death of the cross"* (Philippians 2:8), and now our sins were atoned for, or covered, with His own precious blood. His life for our life—that is what the Father demanded. After it was accomplished, the Father then looked, not on our sin, but on His Son's blood. That was enough; His Son had offered His life in His blood for all mankind. The Father had respect for the pure offering, and our redemption was made complete.

If we honor the blood of Jesus Christ, the Father will smile upon us with forgiveness and cleansing. However, this must not be a dull theological formality, but an active, vital embracing of His blood. We do not offer our own works; we offer only His blood. When God sees the blood of His Son, which we offer as our covering, pardon, and plea, God does not see our sin at all; He can see only the covering, the precious blood of Jesus. Therefore, we understand that *"it is the blood that maketh an atonement for the soul"* (Leviticus 17:11).

three

The Blood Speaks

When Lester Sumrall ministered deliverance to a demon-possessed girl in the Philippine Islands a number of years ago, the demon in the girl spoke in the purest English, although the girl herself spoke only a local dialect. This demon spirit first cursed the Father, then the Son, then the Holy Spirit, and then the blood of Jesus, in that order. I heard Brother Sumrall say at the 1957 Full Gospel Businessmen's Convention in Chicago that the way the demon cursed, it almost seemed that the demon believed the blood of Jesus was alive.

SPEAKING OUT

A so-called Christian lady threw a real tantrum one day and rebuked me severely. But I determined that I was not going to be rebuked by a backslidden woman! I therefore commanded the demon to come out of her. It did—at least one of them did—and caught me by the throat and started to strangle me.

I cried, "The blood!" three times, and the demon went back into her.

But while it tried to choke me, the demon in the lady said, "There you are, *you* have a demon!" But it was a lie of Satan. And, through the blood, I overcame the demon.

On another occasion, I experienced a demonic attack while I slept. In the middle of the night, I awoke to realize that the life had nearly been choked out of me. My heart was strongly oppressed. I felt as if life was almost gone.

I cried, "The blood!" three times. The demon departed rapidly, and the rest of the night was spent in peace. The next night at the same time, the same experience happened to my wife, and the same usage of the blood brought instant deliverance. No demon can get through the blood, but it has to be in place by faith.[3]

DEMONIC REACTIONS

Remembering that the life of God is in the blood of Jesus, I am not surprised at the reaction of these strong demon spirits. As soon as any Christian takes the precious blood of Jesus on his tongue and sings it, talks it, or pleads it, the devil gets terribly disturbed. The devil understands the power of the blood of Jesus, and he has done everything possible to blind Christians to this truth. Many people who are Christians in name only will have nothing to do with what they call "a slaughterhouse religion." Theirs is a religion without the life of God in it, and the devil has no objection to their participating in this kind of religion. But as soon as we honor the blood of Jesus in an active sense, we stir up demons to a fever pitch. It is like fire in a hornet's nest.

It is surprising that so little has been taught about the blood and so little is known about the activity of demon spirits, even within the Christian church. No wise Christian would dare try to cast out demons without faith in the blood of Jesus. I have been used of God many times to deliver people from demon powers, both in soul and body, but never without a conscious pleading of the blood of Jesus and a knowledge that I have been literally covered by His blood. In such cases, Jesus' promise that *"nothing shall by any means hurt you"* (Luke 10:19) and the promise in Isaiah 54:17 that *"no weapon that is formed against thee shall prosper"* find their complete realization.

THE CRY OF JESUS' BLOOD

The protection afforded us by the blood rests in the fact that Jesus' blood says something to

God. The blood cries out to God, "Sin is covered! The penalty is paid!"

In fact, there is abundant evidence in the Bible that all shed blood speaks to God. After the murder of Abel by his brother Cain, we read in Genesis 4:10, *"And* [the Lord] *said, What hast thou done? the voice of thy brother's blood crieth unto me from the ground."* It is clear from this Scripture that the life that was in Abel's blood did not cease after his murder, but cried out for vengeance. This may be difficult for us to grasp, but there is no doubt that God is telling us that innocently shed blood cries out to Him.

In Hebrews 12:24, the writer referred to the blood of Jesus by contrasting it with Abel's blood and calling it *"the blood of sprinkling, that speaketh better things than that of Abel."* Whereas Abel's blood cried out for vengeance, Jesus' blood cries out for mercy. This is what was symbolized in Old Testament days when the mercy seat within the Holy of Holies was sprinkled with the blood of bulls and goats when the high priest went within the veil once a year (Hebrews 9:25).

WITHIN THE VEIL

The result of such sprinkling was that God manifested His *shekinah* glory and spoke to the high priest from between the two cherubim that overshadowed the mercy seat (Exodus 25:22). It is interesting to note that the glory was *seen* and the voice *heard* only when the blood was used. It was not sufficient that the high priest had faith in the blood for the atoning of the sins of Israel for the past year; he had to use it. It is exactly so today. None of us can enter into this holy place (heaven itself) except

> *...by the blood of Jesus, by a new and living way which he hath consecrated for us, through the veil, that is to say, his flesh; and having an high priest over the house of God; let us draw near with a true heart in full assurance of faith, having our hearts sprinkled from an evil conscience, and our bodies washed with pure water.*
> (Hebrews 10:19–22)

When the high priest in the Old Testament went into the Holy of Holies, he would have been stricken dead had he not offered blood. So he carefully offered nothing else but blood. Today in Christian circles, we find many offering other things— works, emotion, *"strange fire"* (Leviticus 10:1), and various kinds of worship—but we must be aware that if we are to enter into *"heavenly places in Christ*

To enter the Holy of Holies, we must offer Jesus' blood.

47

Jesus" (Ephesians 2:6), we can do so only as we consciously offer the blood of Jesus as our only plea.

To plead the blood of Jesus is to confess to God that we are depending wholly on His mercy. As the wonderful old hymn says,

> Rock of Ages, cleft for me,
> Let me hide myself in Thee.
> Let the water and the blood,
> From Thy wounded side which flowed,
> Be of sin the double cure,
> Save from wrath and make me pure.
>
> Nothing in my hand I bring,
> Simply to Thy cross I cling;
> Naked come to Thee for dress,
> Helpless look to Thee for grace;
> Foul I to the fountain fly,
> Wash me Savior or I die.
> (Augustus M. Toplady, 1776)

When we plead the blood of Jesus, it immediately pleads for us, because it is speaking blood, as we have just seen. It speaks mercy from the mercy seat in heaven where Jesus is seated with His Father. This is why we plead the blood of Jesus.

We are convinced that the whole church has yet to learn the value of using the blood of Jesus.

To those who have discovered this secret, the whole realm of God's power is opened, and all the angels in heaven come to help and rescue the child of God who honors, uses, and pleads the blood of Jesus. Truly, "The Spirit answers to the blood," as the songwriter Charles Wesley penned in the old hymn, "Arise, My Soul, Arise."

four

The Passover

The book of Genesis teaches us that the ancient patriarchs offered animals as sacrifices. Abram offered a ram instead of his son Isaac (Genesis 22:13), and Noah built an altar after the flood and offered some of every clean beast and fowl that had been safely delivered through the flood (Genesis 8:20). These scarce animals were very valuable; nothing cheap was good enough to be a worthy sacrifice to God.

Many would have suggested that it was wasteful for Noah to kill and offer the animals that God had delivered from drowning. Why not just kneel down and offer a prayer of thanksgiving? Similarly, many today suggest that we would be better off to have less emphasis on the blood and more on worship and prayer. In this, Satan has deceived us. If we would offer the blood of Jesus more and cut some of our long prayers down in size, we might get better answers and have less fear in our hearts! God can receive us and our praise and thanks only on the basis of the blood of His Son. There is no other way into God's presence.

REQUIRED BLOOD SACRIFICES

The children of Israel knew this in Egypt. Although they had no codified law, yet the word had been passed down from generation to generation that God required blood. The Israelites knew about blood because their forefather Abraham had taught them that they owed their very existence as a nation to God's mercy in supplying a ram for sacrifice in place of the life of Isaac. Had Isaac not been spared, there would have been no nation of Israel, for Isaac was Abraham's only son of promise. So Isaac was a miraculously delivered child, saved by the blood of a substitute sacrifice. Every Israelite had been taught this story and understood the importance of the blood.

God taught them this even more dramatically when He delivered them from Egyptian bondage. God had visited nine terrible plagues upon Egypt, but still Pharaoh would not let the children of Israel go. It took blood to turn the battle in favor of God's people.

God said to Moses and Aaron, *"Speak ye unto all the congregation of Israel, saying, In the tenth day of this month they shall take to them every man a lamb,...a lamb for an house"* (Exodus 12:3). It was to be a lamb without blemish, the most expensive one in the flock, nothing cheap or second rate. It was to be the best. Each house was

to have a lamb, and that lamb would count for the whole house—one lamb for about fifteen people. There is tremendous truth here for Christian families. God wants to save entire families, and all Christians ought to claim the salvation of their households!

God wants to save entire families.

Beginning in Exodus 12:7, we read these further instructions:

> *They shall take of the blood, and strike it on the two side posts and on the upper door post of the houses, wherein they shall eat it....For I will pass through the land of Egypt this night, and will smite all the firstborn in the land of Egypt, both man and beast....And the blood shall be to you for a token upon the houses where ye are: and when I see the blood, I will pass over you, and the plague shall not be upon you to destroy you....And ye shall take a bunch of hyssop, and dip it in the blood that is in the basin, and strike the lintel and the two side posts with the blood that is in the basin; and none of you shall go out at the door of his house until the morning. For the LORD will pass through to smite the Egyptians; and when he seeth the blood upon the lintel, and on the two side posts, the LORD will pass over the door, and will*

not suffer the destroyer to come in unto
your houses to smite you.
(Exodus 12:7, 12–13, 22–23)

THERE'S SAFETY IN OBEDIENCE

Several things are to be noted here. First, if any Israelite had made a mockery of these unusual orders given by God through a man, or if anyone had claimed that Moses and Aaron were mad and not capable of leading them any longer, then they would have perished with no second chance. Second, had they decided to "go to another church" where such "rubbish" was not taught, they would have perished. Third, if they had decided to venture out in the middle of the night to see what was going on, even for one brief second, they would have perished, for they would not at that time have been "under the blood." Fourth, if they had decided to offer their own righteousness and not sprinkle the blood, they would have perished. Finally, had they sprinkled tinted water or red paint or some other substance, it would not have been good enough; they would have been smitten dead.

If similar orders were given by God's servants today, very few would even consider obeying! Blood is not a pleasant substance to handle; it is unhygienic in hot weather, attracting flies and germs. No modern sanitary department would agree to such action today. A more practical, sensible, desirable way would need to be found, but surely not blood.

OVERCOMING THE DESTROYER

Notice also that when God surveyed the scene, He would not permit the *"destroyer"* to enter into their homes to visit them with death. Who is this destroyer made helpless by blood? The answer is found in Revelation:

> *And they had a king over them, which is the angel of the bottomless pit, whose name in the Hebrew tongue is Abaddon, but in the Greek tongue hath his name Apollyon.*   (Revelation 9:11)

Both *Abaddon* in Hebrew and *Apollyon* in Greek mean "destroyer." So the great destroyer is none other than Satan, the king of the demons of the bottomless pit.

It is important to understand that Satan is the destroyer. Nothing good or constructive ever comes from him. He is the author of death and misery. But the Bible assures us that God is supreme and that Satan cannot bring destruction and trouble to anyone unless it is permitted by God. And even if God should grant such permission to the destroyer, still He will work out even that for your blessing if you are a Christian

(Romans 8:28). Righteous Job was given boils by Satan. It was Satan who took the lives of his children, destroyed his cattle, and burned up his home—but only with God's permission. Yet God worked it out for Job's good in the end: *"And the LORD turned the captivity of Job, when he prayed for his friends: also the LORD gave Job twice as much as he had before"* (Job 42:10).

Satan is both the ruler of this world system and the prince of the upper atmosphere that surrounds this earth (John 12:31; Ephesians 2:2). It is only the mercy of God that keeps us from the incredible power of the wicked destroying angel, Satan. It is only faith in the blood of Jesus that comes between us, the devil, and his demon spirits.

SAVING ENTIRE HOUSEHOLDS

If it had not been for the blood sprinkled on the lintels and doorposts of the homes of the Israelites, the firstborn in every family would have perished. Even the cattle were saved by blood. What a wonderful truth for faithful tithing farmers today! If you reckon by faith that the blood of Jesus avails for your home and your cattle, it will do so, and the angel of death will just as surely be kept away from you and yours!

We have been told that it is not scriptural to pray for cattle, but we have seen cows and even dogs healed with the laying on of hands! It was somewhere around 1910 that the late John G. Lake was challenged to pray for a horse that was bleeding to death in the streets of Johannesburg, South Africa. He accepted the challenge and began to rebuke the flow of blood. Immediately the blood stopped, and the horse got up to its feet and lived. How was this miracle brought about? By pleading the blood of Jesus.

COVERING OUR CHILDREN

I have found many young babies who were extremely irritable and frequently wore out their mothers. Only when we prayed for them were they delivered. Babies and young children rarely have any noticeable reactions during deliverance. The demon probably has not sunk deeply into the personality of the child, and therefore it easily yields to an authoritative command in the Lord's name.

Demons may also enter young children. Many adults have testified that a terribly frightening experience as a young child gave opportunity for the evil spirit to come in. Having entered, the spirit will not leave readily, especially when a person waits fifty years before seeking deliverance.

During this period of time, the spirit digs in more and more tenaciously and may bring other symptoms such as fear, pains, arthritis, and stomach disorders. To prevent such demonic attacks in childhood, Christian parents should ask God's protection for their children each night and ask for a covering of the blood of Jesus.[4]

It all gets back to the word *atonement*, which means "a covering." When the Israelites used the blood, taking hyssop and splashing the blood upon their lintels and doorposts (Exodus 12:22), God would not permit Satan or his demon spirits to enter their homes. The Israelites were completely covered. Satan, that teeth-gnashing creature, was bound in fury by God because the Israelites used blood. I believe the reason that so many Christians are feeble, sick, and fearful today is because they have not been taught to use the blood of Jesus as a covering.

PENTECOSTAL REVIVAL EXPERIENCES

In the early days of the Pentecostal revival, between 1908 and 1912, much was heard about "pleading the blood." Mrs. Woodworth-Etter, in her great deliverance campaigns in Los Angeles and Chicago, used to stand with hands raised and by living faith sprinkle the blood of Jesus upon the crowds. The results described in her book are fantastic. People would come rushing to the front of the auditorium and fall prostrate; many were healed before they reached the front; many fell down speaking in other tongues. Such songs as "We Are under the Blood" were sung frequently in those days.

In the early days of the outpouring of the Spirit in Great Britain, such marvelous baptisms of the Spirit were experienced through pleading the blood that people came from all over the world to receive their baptism.

It is recorded in Pastor Kent White's book, *The Word of God Coming Again* (now out of print), that the reality of using the blood by speaking it or pleading it came by sovereign revelation of the Holy Spirit to hungry seekers. Previous to that time, not much was known about

When we plead the blood, the devil must flee.

the importance of pleading the blood. Even a young girl of tender years was heard pleading the blood earnestly under a table! No one had taught her about this; it came to her as a revelation from the Holy Spirit. As soon as this truth was discovered by more people, the number of those receiving true baptisms in the Spirit increased greatly.

One of the best-known places where such experiences were received was in the Parish Hall of St. Mary's Church near Sunderland, England, where the Church of England vicar, A. A. Boddy, was conducting Holy Spirit meetings. Smith Wigglesworth received his baptism of the Spirit there. Nonetheless, after some time, the practice of pleading the blood for the baptism died out, to be replaced by praising and other methods. However, it was recorded that the number receiving the baptism dropped off considerably, until a brother from a Scottish assembly in Kilsyth came down and urged them to honor the blood in their seeking once again. Immediately the power of God fell afresh, and people were prostrated under the power of God, speaking in tongues. Even Vicar Boddy was stricken under the power of God.

Is it any wonder that mighty miracles were commonplace in those days? Is it any wonder that divine healing came in as a tremendous revelation? When folks started to plead the blood, the devil just had to leave. Satan cannot stand before the blood of Jesus when it is honored.

THE ULTIMATE WEAPON

I am convinced that when people cannot receive a good clear baptism in the Holy Spirit, it is because they are bound by Satan. In such cases, the best and most scriptural way of obtaining release is to go into the presence of God boldly

pleading the blood of Jesus out loud, opening one's whole soul to the incoming of the Spirit.

Some may argue that this is not a scriptural practice for New Testament Christians. But let me refer you to Hebrews where we read that we *"are come...to the blood of sprinkling"* (Hebrews 12:22, 24). This does not refer back to the past, but is a present-tense experience, *"we **are** come."* It is our privilege now as New Testament priests of the *"church of the firstborn"* (v. 23) to sprinkle the blood of Jesus—not merely to believe that Jesus did it for us in the past (which He certainly did), but to do it now. We must now battle the

> *As New Testament priests, we are to sprinkle the blood of Jesus.*

principalities and powers and wicked spirits of the devil (Ephesians 6:12); thus we sprinkle that precious blood once shed for us, and Satan and his demon powers must give ground. They may be stubborn, but Christians should be even more stubborn. We possess the winning weapons!

Because the enemy is tenacious, the victory does not always come easily. Sometimes we need to battle with the weapon of the blood in prayer for weeks and months. But victory is certain. In Revelation 12:11, we read of saints who overcame

Satan *"by the blood of the Lamb, and by the word of their testimony."* No hint is given of the possibility of failure. *"They overcame."* And they accomplished this by the blood and by their testimony.

Peter also gave some good teaching on this subject. We are *"elect...unto obedience and sprinkling of the blood of Jesus Christ"* (1 Peter 1:2). It is not a passive faith in the blood that brings victory, but an active sprinkling of it in faith by each elect believer. Peter continued the theme by telling us that, as holy priests, we are *"to offer up spiritual sacrifices, acceptable to God by Jesus Christ"* (1 Peter 2:5). As the priests offered up daily blood sacrifices on behalf of the people in Old Testament times, so also today in New Testament times we offer the blood of Jesus Christ to God as our plea on behalf of ourselves, our children, our loved ones, and even our livestock!

OBEDIENCE AND EFFECTIVENESS

Mrs. Nuzum, a Pentecostal author of the early part of the twentieth century, wrote much on the subject of covering our loved ones with the blood of Jesus. I can tell you that even in my own family this practice has been most usable and effective during the past twenty years. And there are many others who likewise testify of its effectiveness. Great peace of mind and wonderful answers to

prayer have come to those who practice using the blood as a covering.

The destroyer cannot get in under the bloodline where it has been placed. But, unfortunately, too many have been loosely taught that Satan cannot ever get through the bloodline. They have not been informed that Satan can and does get through if the bloodline is let down. And how do we let it down? By our disobedience.

We can hardly claim to be under the blood of Jesus if we are walking in deliberate disobedience. Peter stated that we are *"elect…unto obedience and sprinkling of the blood of Jesus"* (1 Peter 1:2). Sprinkling or pleading the blood of Jesus without obedience to the Word of God will avail us nothing. Remember that if an Israelite had come out of his home for a moment during the night of the Passover, he would have died within sight of the blood simply because it was not covering him at that instant! He would have believed in the blood all right, but he would not have been honoring it in obedience. In like manner, the New Testament makes it clear that we must sprinkle the blood of Jesus in faith and with obedience.

five

The Scarlet Thread

In the second chapter of Joshua, the story of the harlot Rahab and the two Israelite spies in the city of Jericho is a remarkable account of deliverance through blood. The scarlet thread was a token of blood.

Israel was commanded to go in and take the wicked city because it was wholly given over to sin. It is perhaps difficult for us in Western cities to appreciate how low and debauched some cities became in early Bible times. For instance, the city of Sodom, which was eventually destroyed, was so base that even angels were accosted by the men of the city for purposes of moral perversion. We have no reason to believe that Jericho was much better. The two spies found shelter in a harlot's house, and it seems probable that this woman supported her father, mother, brothers, and sisters by prostitution. It is also highly probable that her brothers were "pimps" and that her sisters engaged in the same traffic. So these two children of God found refuge in the best place they could find—a brothel! Is it any wonder that God desired to wipe the memory of such a wicked city from the face of the earth? And He chose His people Israel as the instruments for that purpose.

REPENTANCE AND FAITH

As soon as the two men of God arrived, Rahab began to feel the need of repentance. Her conscience began bothering her a great deal. She had heard of the fame of the God of Israel, and upon being faced with her guilt, she began to confess her faith in Him: *"For the LORD your God, he is God in heaven above, and in earth beneath"* (Joshua 2:11). She asked them to help her stay alive, for she knew by revelation of the Spirit that Israel would surely win the battle and destroy Jericho. She wanted to be left alive with her whole house. But how could it be done? *"Give me a true token"* (v. 12), she said.

It didn't take her long to find out that God is always willing to reveal Himself to those who really want to know Him. She was willing to comply with the instructions of the two children of God. She was willing to start living a new life of faith in God. So the two spies promised, by the God of Israel, that they would indeed save her life, and her father, mother, brothers, and sisters—in fact, all who were inside that house on the walls of Jericho.

Because of Rahab's faith, the Lamb of God *"slain from the foundation of the world"* (Revelation 13:8) became efficacious for this poor harlot and her sinning family. Perhaps it seems strange to you that such a woman should be saved, but God's dealings with sinners are always quite unbelievable! Jesus has no appeal to the worldly-wise and the self-righteous. He came to those who have need of a physician (Mark 2:17). Here was a poor woman who knew that she had need of God, and He was ready to forgive her immediately!

STAY UNDER THE BLOOD'S PROTECTION

The two spies remembered that the blood that had been sprinkled on the lintels and doorposts of their homes in Egypt had been given to them as a token (Exodus 12:13). It spoke of the blood of Jesus, already shed in the mind of the Father. Had they been able, I am sure those two spies would have slain a lamb and sprinkled its blood on Rahab's home. But there was no time for that. The king of Jericho, who knew of their presence in the city, was searching for them. They had no time to slay a lamb and do what Moses had done, so they said to Rahab, "We will give you a token; take this scarlet cord and tie it in your window" (Joshua 2:18). They told her that if she would do this, symbolically honoring the blood, that her whole house would be preserved and her loved ones would walk out alive, even if everyone else in Jericho perished. But there was one condition. "Stay in your house," they said. "If any go out, their blood will be on their own heads" (v. 19). But absolute safety was promised to those who would stay in the house, under the protection of the blood.

This showed amazing faith on the part of the two spies, who were able to prophetically promise such a remarkable thing. They had faith in the blood! And the Bible tells us that Rahab did what she was told in complete faith and simplicity: *"According unto your words, so be it.... and she bound the scarlet line in the window"* (Joshua 2:21). Yes, there is a bloodline, and the great destroyer cannot get through it; but have you drawn it around your situation?

Is your house under the protection of the blood?

We know the story so well. The Israelites, led by their singers, walked around the walls of Jericho for seven days. On the seventh day, they walked around seven times. Then God did His part. Never expect God to do His part until you have done what you know to do! God sent the earthquake. It broke down the walls of the city. The Israelites then entered in and set fire to it, killing right and left; but the section of the wall on which Rahab's house was built remained intact. Her house was untouched. With her whole family, she walked out alive and joined God's people. Gentiles were permitted into the house of Israel by faith in Israel's God, and the blood of Jesus availed for them even then.

Note particularly that if Rahab had not been obedient in the details given by the spies, she and her family would have perished. It was the token of the bloodline that saved them; for when God saw this scarlet thread, He passed over the house and did not suffer the destroyer to enter in. A miracle indeed! Rahab used the blood, not in passive faith, but in active faith that gets results.

DEDICATION FOR THE PRIESTHOOD

Even many years before this, when the high priest and his sons were ordained to the priesthood, part of their ordination included putting blood upon (1) the lobes of their right ears, (2) the thumbs of their right hands, and (3) the big toes of their right feet (Leviticus 8:23–24). Thus, in type, Israel was taught that the blood cleanses and sanctifies all that enters into a man's ear, everything he puts his hand to do, and wherever he goes in the course of his duties. Even if he walks into a den of vice (not to partake of it!), the blood will keep Satan away from his thought life, his work life, and wherever he goes.

Remembering the teaching given by the apostle Paul that our bodies are temples of the Holy Spirit (2 Corinthians 6:16) and that we are not to deliberately touch any unclean thing, it is interesting to realize that as *"priests of God and of Christ"* (Revelation 20:6), we can also apply Christ's precious blood to our ears, thumbs, and toes and know that our whole lives—spirit, soul, and body—will *"be preserved blameless unto the coming of our Lord Jesus Christ"* (1 Thessalonians 5:23).

ACTIVATE YOUR FAITH IN THE BLOOD

I repeat, I am convinced that the reason so many Christians are living such miserable lives, with sickness and recurring sin, is that they have not realized we must turn our passive theological faith in the blood into a vital, active faith that uses it, sprinkles it, pleads it, and recognizes that it is just as effective today when applied in faith as it was in the days of Moses and Joshua.

When the blood covers us and we know it— and we have placed it by faith upon our hearts, lives, homes, and loved ones—then we have created a condition where Satan cannot get through. So keep under the blood! This is one substance that all the devils in hell cannot penetrate. But, it is not there automatically. Salvation is not automatic. Healing for the body is not automatic. No promise of God is obtained automatically, but all the promises are obtained through faith and maintained by continuing in that faith. We are not to let down our faith in the blood. There is more power in the blood than anyone has ever imagined.

EMERGENCY CIRCUMSTANCES

In 1945, our third son was born. As a baby, he was fed on a kind of thin, hot porridge that my wife prepared for him. This was heated to the temperature of boiling water (212° F). As she was taking this upstairs, carrying the cup in one hand and a large jug of boiling water in the other, in her haste she tripped on a step. Thinking first to save her legs from the boiling water, she managed to place the jug on a step safely. But in so doing, she spilled the hot cereal, and it spread over her arm, settling in the crook of her elbow. It is obvious that boiling porridge would produce a bad burn on such a sensitive spot and cause the skin to peel off and inflammation to set in. When the porridge was wiped off, her arm was red and painful. However, the baby had to be bathed and fed, and there was no one to help. So my wife began to plead the blood of Jesus out loud several times, believing that it was applied to her injured arm. After a few minutes, the pain left, and she was able to bathe and feed the baby. That same evening, all that could be seen was a small red mark about the size of a dime where the center of the burn had been. By the next morning, no trace of red could be seen at all. Her flesh and skin were perfectly whole.

We must realize that Satan is the author of all damage to the body. Demons try to attack any injured part of our body and permit germs, which are always around us, to impinge on the injured flesh and do their work of destruction and poisoning. But when the blood of Jesus is applied in faith, it acts as a covering that prevents Satan from attacking us with germs. Therefore, the natural healing processes in our body quickly do their work because they are not hindered by Satan. The blood of Jesus is the finest covering and disinfectant in the world. It is perfect.

WITHOUT A SCRATCH

The power of Jesus' blood was vividly demonstrated one day when we were traveling in Canada. We had as passengers a young married couple whom we were bringing back to Toronto with us. We had told them about the wonderful truths concerning pleading the blood of Jesus. Little did we know, as we drove along in the rain, that God had a plan whereby we were going to demonstrate this truth to save our lives. Coming over a rise on the road, we hit some bad potholes. The back wheels, which were under coiled springs, went into a bounce. The car literally jigged and skidded to the wrong side of the road, completely out of control. Before us we could see three cars approaching at about 60 M.P.H., and we were powerless to avoid a terrible crash. Immediately we started to plead the blood of Jesus out loud.

The blood of Jesus can cover you in times of trouble.

Our friends in the backseat, who had been sound asleep, suddenly awoke, realizing that something was wrong. It seemed that an angel of the Lord then took over. The back wheels suddenly gripped and stopped bouncing, and the car returned to the right side of the road and went off the pavement with the front wheels down in a grassy ditch. We thought we could possibly pull out of the ditch and back onto the road. But the grass was too soft due to the rain, and we found that we were stuck.

What now? We were safe, we were alive, but we were stuck. So God still had more to do on behalf of His servants. He had said, *"Call upon me in the day of trouble: I will deliver thee, and thou shalt glorify me"* (Psalm 50:15). So we did this, and almost immediately two men drove up in an old car. We said nothing, but one of them said, "We will pull you out." They put action to their words and pulled a chain out of the trunk, attached it to our car, and pulled us safely out of the ditch. We were safely delivered from death, without a scratch on our bodies or our car. Why? The blood of Jesus covered us because we put it there by faith!

A SPIRIT OF SUICIDE

Around that time, a Christian brother, who had been a deacon in a full gospel church, was battling a strong urge to commit suicide. Could it be that a Holy Spirit-baptized man—a deacon in a full gospel assembly—could be demon possessed?

What would our Bible schools say? What would the pastor of his church say? What would anyone say? Who cares what they say! I quickly told the afflicted man that demons were probably the source of his torment. Being desperate, he asked what he could do. Remembering a recent deliverance session where an asthmatic was gloriously set free, I felt I was ready for anything.

"There is one thing we can do," I said. "We can cast out these suicide demons."

"When?" he asked.

"Tonight," I replied, full of faith and the joy of the Lord! I was learning that I was seated in heavenly places in Christ and had been given authority over demonic forces.

My wife came down into the basement kitchen with us. We sat on one side of the room, and this despondent man sat on the other side with his wife. The kitchen became an arena of spiritual battle.

We began by singing choruses about the blood of Jesus because we didn't want these demons to attack us. There is nothing like a fresh reminder of the power of Jesus' blood. The demons knew they had no power over us. Then we gave the command.

Nothing compares to the power of Jesus' blood.

To my astonishment, this man shot into the air about one foot off his chair. He landed with a thud, and his head shook to and fro like a toy in a dog's mouth.

We doubled our forceful commands in the name of Jesus and ordered every foul suicide demon to come out. After one hour, many unclean spirits had come out moaning, coughing, vomiting, and writhing. Then they started to speak. We had read about demons who spoke to Jesus, but we didn't know anyone who heard demons speak today. We know differently now.

We asked the spirits how many more remained in our brother, and they replied, "Twenty." We counted them as they came out, paused at each fifth one, and asked again. Amazingly, they told the truth, although they argued and sometimes refused to answer. But our pressing commands in Jesus' name caused them to tell the truth.

"Fifteen." "Ten." "Five." The last demon put up a twenty-minute fight, but the name of Jesus, His precious blood, and an authoritative command expelled him. Finally set free from demonic bondage, this brother threw his head back and spoke in tongues, magnifying God.

He then made a pact with God; he said that if he was truly delivered, he would like God to give him the gift of prophecy. The next Sunday around the communion table, this cleansed vessel brought forth a beautiful prophetic word that edified the entire church.

"IS THERE HOPE FOR ME?"

Perhaps the best Scripture on this subject details the story of the man whose house was garnished, swept, and cleansed after the evil spirit had gone out. This demon was not so easily defeated. He wandered around, waiting for a convenient moment to return. Finally, the man backslid, and the demon did return and brought with him seven other spirits worse than himself. (See Matthew 12:43–45.)

To say that this man was not saved is to misuse the plain meaning of words. Obviously, he was saved, delivered, and cleansed in the blood; but he chose to backslide and consequently returned to his previous habit, and seven other demons came to plague him. The frightful possibility of such a relapse was made very real to me a number of years ago.

The telephone rang. "Is that you, Pastor Whyte?" The same man who had been delivered from twenty demons in our church kitchen seven years before was on the line.

"Yes," I replied. "What can I do for you?"

"Are you in the same place?"

"Yes."

"Do you still have the same ministry?"

"Yes."

He sighed with relief, saying that God had directed him to call me. He was trapped in the pit of sin again. "Do you think there's any hope for me?" he sighed. "I'm in a terrible mess."

I assured him that there was indeed hope, for the mercies of God are new every morning. So he came to my office.

His story was very sordid but a warning to us all. After his spectacular deliverance, he had moved out of the area and into the suburbs. The new church he attended did not believe the full gospel and did not teach or practice healing or deliverance.

One rainy day, as he drove downtown to his business in Toronto, he noticed a man at a bus stop. With compassion, he invited the man to get into his car. This worldly man offered our friend a cigarette. His offer opened a wonderful opportunity for our friend to witness about the salvation and deliverance available in Christ. But no. Instead, he took the cigarette, which proved to be his first step to hell on earth.

Each day he picked up this man, and each day they smoked. Soon they talked about drinking together. Their sin escalated from the tavern to the racetrack where they bet on the horses. Finally, the newfound friend said to our brother, "I love you."

As I listened to this man's story, I could hardly believe it. He had a beautiful wife, four wonderful children, and a good home. I had often visited them. What power drove a good Christian man to become a homosexual, leave his wife and family, and live in one room with another man? Psychology cannot explain this. It was the devil working through indwelling demons.

WORSE OFF THAN BEFORE

Theology explains that no Christian can have a demon. But I remembered how God had delivered this dear brother from a demon of suicide seven years before. How could this Spirit-filled man have gotten a suicide demon in the first place? And what about the demons that were in him now?

I knew there was only one answer. He had arrived at this miserable state by disobeying the words of Scripture: *"Neither give place to the devil"* (Ephesians 4:27). He had allowed the devil to occupy territory that had previously been occupied by the Holy Spirit.

The broken man slumped into a chair after his agonizing confession. He had scraped the bottom of the barrel of sin but was ready to be rescued again.

Without further delay, we gave the command. "Come out, in the name of Jesus!" The man was ready. The filthy demons began to pour out of him with almost continual coughing and choking. Without any asking on my part, they willingly named themselves as they came out. Lust, filth, uncleanness, perversion, cursing, etc. In twenty minutes he was completely free again.

When it was all over, I realized that I had seen a fulfillment of Jesus' words:

When the unclean spirit is gone out of a man, he walketh through dry places, seeking rest, and findeth none. Then he saith, I will return into my house from whence I came out; and when he is come, he findeth it empty, swept, and garnished. Then goeth he, and taketh with himself seven other spirits more wicked than himself, and they enter in and dwell there: and the last state of that man is worse than the first.
(Matthew 12:43–45)

This explained what had happened to the man. After his first deliverance, his "house" had been cleansed, swept, and put in order, but he had not kept it filled with the new Visitor, the Holy Spirit. His house had been left empty, so the suicide spirit came back. However, that spirit also beckoned to seven of his filthy friends, and they came in also. What a mess a Christian can get himself into by backsliding! But thank God, deliverance is available to all who will bend the knee to Jesus and ask Him to forgive their sins and enter into their lives.

FULLY RESTORED

Seven years later, I met this same brother again in a certain church. Immediately I asked how he was doing. He joyfully told me that after his second deliverance, he returned home and made a full confession to his wife and family. They forgave him and took him back. God then began to prosper his business, and he bought a better home. He was keeping his house clean with the blood of Jesus, and the demons had permanently left.[5]

six

The Value of the Blood

A
ny attempt to appraise the value of the blood of Christ would be impossible. It is priceless! We learn from 1 Corinthians 6:20 and 7:23 that we are *"bought with a price,"* and that price is the blood of Jesus, which Peter called *"precious."* Don't you remember how he said, *"Ye were not redeemed with corruptible things, as silver and gold...but with the precious blood of Christ"* (1 Peter 1:18–19)?

AT THE TEMPLE DEDICATION

When the temple was dedicated on Mount Moriah, the actual count of animals slaughtered was amazing. Before the ark of the covenant was brought in, it is recorded that the sacrificing of sheep and oxen *"could not be told nor numbered for multitude"* (1 Kings 8:5; 2 Chronicles 5:6). Scripture further tells us that a peace offering was later made on behalf of the whole nation of Israel, and it is recorded that 22,000 oxen and 120,000 sheep were sacrificed, and *"so the king and all the children of Israel dedicated the house of the LORD"* (1 Kings 8:63). Furthermore, we must remember that only the best animals were accepted for sacrifice by the Levites. No "seconds" were good enough. Doesn't this seem to be a ridiculous, senseless waste? Wouldn't one sheep or a small inexpensive lamb have been enough? Surely, if God wanted to keep the symbolism right, one little lamb would have been enough to typify the Lamb of God who took away the sins of the world!

But, no, 22,000 oxen, worth hundreds of dollars apiece, and 120,000 sheep had to die. By this, I believe God is trying to impress upon us that the value of the blood cannot be measured in dollars, cents, or gallons. No amount of blood of animals in the Old Testament could have atoned for your sins and mine. On the Day of Atonement, the blood of the animal sacrifices flowed continually from the altar for days, as a sign of the promise to the inhabitants of Jerusalem that when God would cause His Son to die sacrificially, He would open a fountain that will flow forever. (See Zechariah 13:1.) This is a continually flowing river into which we may plunge daily to wash away our sins and

> *No amount of animal sacrifices could atone for sin.*

sicknesses and sorrows. This stream ever flows before Satan and all his host; and as we honor it, sing about it, talk about it, and plead it out loud, the blood of Jesus pleads mercy, forgiveness, pardon, healing, protection, deliverance, and multiplied joy and peace.

DAILY SACRIFICES

It is not enough to believe in the historic blood of Calvary. It is necessary that we believe in the fountain now, and by faith avail ourselves of its power and life. Love is only a word until it is demonstrated; and in like manner, blood is only a word until it is used. Ammunition in an arsenal is useless. It must be taken and *used* to bring terror to the enemy. The army of the Lord is powerless until it uses its weapons, which are *"mighty through God to the pulling down of strong holds"* (2 Corinthians 10:4). The primary weapons are the sword of the Spirit, which is the Word of God, and the blood, for we read in Revelation 12:11, *"They overcame him* [Satan] *by the blood of the Lamb, and by the word of their testimony."* We need the Word and the blood.

We must remember that the sacrifices of blood made by King Solomon did not end the sacrifices. There were daily sacrifices, to remind the people of the present power and efficacy of the blood. Yesterday's leftovers could not be accepted.

We get the same thought with the manna, which speaks of the Word of God. Only what was picked up that day was sweet and suitable for use. In like manner, the blood of Jesus is fresh and sweet today—not dead and coagulated. The daily shedding of blood should bring home to us the tremendous value that God places on blood: *"Without shedding of blood is no remission"* (Hebrews 9:22).

THE SYMBOLISM OF THE OLD COVENANT SACRIFICES

The blood offerings were tremendous, and they should prove to us the tremendous meaning and value of the blood of the Lamb of God. The great Day of Atonement, held annually, with the scapegoat taken off into the wilderness, had great meaning as a type of Christ, who took the condemnation and curse of sin upon Himself and carried it off into an uninhabited desert place, to be seen no more (Leviticus 16:10, 21–22).

The sin offering represented the broken covenant between God and man, caused by man's original fall into sin. Again we see that God and man can be reconciled only by blood. There were daily and evening sacrifices, with a double burnt offering on the Sabbath, as well as the burnt offerings on the great festivals or special Sabbaths. All these foreshadowed Jesus Christ, who made a full surrender of His life by pouring out His blood—a perfect sacrifice in our stead, consumed in the fiery heat of His great sufferings for us.

The value of the blood is also taught by the great number of lambs slaughtered in the annual observance of the Passover. In this annual event, the head of each family would bring a lamb for sacrifice unto the Lord. According to Josephus (*Wars* VI, 9, 3), ten people was the least number and twenty the greatest permissible number of individuals who could partake of a single Passover lamb. If one lamb was slain for fifteen people on an average throughout the

Jesus was a perfect sacrifice in our stead.

nation, then for the 2.5 million people at the time of the Exodus, over 160,000 lambs were slain on that historic night when the bonds of Egypt gave way before the blood.

In the time of Solomon, the population had increased to five or six million, so the great slaughter of lambs, by all who were able to take part, may be estimated to be around 400,000. What would our hard-pressed farmers say today if such a large number were required for sacrifice annually? But thank God, we read in

1 Corinthians 5:7 that *"Christ our passover is sacrificed for us."* No longer are we expected to take a lamb for fifteen people and offer its blood for our sins and sicknesses, for Christ took our place and became our Passover Lamb. We now accept His singular, pure, perfect sacrifice (Hebrews 10:9–14) and offer His blood by faith.

If every Christian who names the name of Jesus would plead His precious blood every day— out loud—we believe that the result would be catastrophic in Satan's kingdom and that great deliverance would be felt in the church and in the nation.

GUARDING YOUR BLOOD-BOUGHT DELIVERANCE

However, I need to emphasize the fact that any deliverance brought about through the pleading of the blood can be maintained only as the parties concerned meet the conditions for keeping that deliverance. An arresting example of this fact took place in Cadillac, Michigan, where I was conducting special services. One evening, a compassionate Christian woman brought with her a four-year-old girl whose eyes were badly crossed.

"Brother Whyte," she said, "this little girl's parents are unbelievers. Will you pray for her

eyes? Perhaps if God heals this child, her parents will be awakened."

So we removed the child's glasses and prayed for her. I removed the curse by pleading the blood. Immediately her eyes straightened out, to the amazement of everyone present. Needless to say, there were many tear-filled eyes in that congregation as the little girl, who had previously seen only double, toddled around the church saying, "I see one! I see one!"

Deliverance cannot be maintained without the blood.

However, when the kind Christian woman took her back to her unbelieving parents and told them what had happened, they refused to believe it.

"You get those glasses back on!" her father said to her. "We're not having any of that nonsense around here!" And they forced the girl to wear the glasses. By their unbelief, they destroyed the faith of the little child, and through time, her eyes became crossed again.

So it is clear that no deliverance can be maintained without keeping under the blood. But as long as we stay under the blood by faith and obedience, Satan cannot penetrate the bloodline. No wonder we say that the blood of Jesus is of such infinite value!

A SINGULAR OFFERING

It is impossible to compute the amount of blood that was shed in the 1,500 years of Israel's history under the old covenant. Nothing could be obtained from God except on the basis of blood sacrifice, nor can anything be obtained today except on the basis of the blood of Jesus, which flows as a healing stream for the spirit, soul, and body of man.

Very shortly after the resurrection of Jesus, He appeared to Mary before He appeared to anyone else and said to her, *"Touch me not; for I am not yet ascended to my Father"* (John 20:17). In the law of Israel, a high priest could not be touched by the people just before he entered into the Holy Place with the blood of animals; it was only after he had offered blood and been accepted before the mercy seat that the common people could touch him.

In like manner, Jesus the High Priest could not be touched with human hands until He had ascended to His Father and offered His blood at the throne of God. (See Hebrews 9.) We assume this was done sometime soon after He appeared to Mary, for when He appeared to the other disciples a few days later, He said, *"Behold my hands and my feet, that it is I myself: handle me, and see; for a spirit hath not flesh and bones, as ye see me have"* (Luke 24:39). So apparently, the sprinkling of His blood had been accomplished by that time.

ENTER BOLDLY

We know that the high priest entered once a year into the Holy Place with blood (Hebrews 9:7–14). If he had entered into the Holy of Holies without blood, he would have been stricken dead instantly. However, the offering and sprinkling of the blood on the mercy seat caused the miraculous *shekinah* glory of God to light up the darkened room, and God then communed with the high priest above the mercy seat (Exodus 25:22).

To fulfill this type, we read of Jesus who *"neither by the blood of goats and calves, but by his own blood...entered in once into the holy place, having obtained eternal redemption for us"* (Hebrews 9:12). Just how Jesus transported His own precious blood from Calvary to heaven is not understood by mortal man, but the Scripture shows that He fulfilled the type, and therefore He must have sprinkled His own blood upon the mercy seat (the throne of God) in heaven. This blood was accepted. No other sacrifice would have been sufficient except His precious blood.

Now you and I can enter right into the Holy Place of heaven itself anytime we want to. Anytime we have a need, whether of deliverance or of the baptism of the Spirit, we can enter into the Holy Place of heaven itself. But how? Without blood? A thousand times, no! We can come only with the precious blood of Jesus.

> *Having therefore, brethren, boldness to enter into the holiest by the blood of Jesus, ...let us draw near with a true heart in full assurance of faith, having our hearts sprinkled.* (Hebrews 10:19, 22)

OUR VALUE IN HIM

Jesus said, *"I am...the life"* (John 14:6). Christianity is not an imitation of the life of Christ (even if that were possible). It is not obeying "your church." It is not a monastic life of suppressing natural desires and appetites. It is a life of abundance for spirit, soul, and body. Jesus said that He came to give life and to give it more abundantly (John 10:10). He came to take that tired, bound, captive life and fill it with His overwhelming abundance. Can we imagine Adam being sick, depressed, miserable, weak, and fearful in the garden?

Jesus came to give us back everything that Adam lost, and as we shall see, even more under the new covenant in His blood. Abundant life means just what it says for every child of God: Everyone who approaches the mercy seat will immediately have available to him every blessing in the Bible, and there are thousands. Abundant life—including joy, peace, strength, health, and prosperity—is laid to your account in heaven by Jesus Christ. *"My God shall supply all your need according to his riches in glory by Christ Jesus"* (Philippians 4:19).

Unfortunately, when a child of God does venture into the bank of heaven, after knocking timorously instead of walking in boldly as if he owned the place (and he does!), he usually cautiously and apologetically approaches one of the tellers, proffers a check with a small amount, and frankly wonders whether it will be honored! This is not an exaggeration concerning the approach in prayer of the average child of God. We might just as well write "million" as "two" because it belongs to us as heirs of God.

We may approach God boldly, as heirs.

Let us therefore go boldly into the Holiest Place *"by a new and living way"* (Hebrews 10:20), and plead the blood of Jesus as our reason for expecting fantastic blessings. The world uses the word *payoff.* Our payoff includes everything the moment we dare to enjoy it by faith. The blood of Jesus purchased every redemptive blessing for us.

"But I am not worthy of His blessings." Who said so? The opposite is the truth; this is a lie of

Satan. *"Thou hast a few names...which have not defiled their garments; and they shall walk with me in white: for they are worthy"* (Revelation 3:4). Jesus makes us worthy in Him. As long as we abide in Him and permit His words to abide in us, then we will continue to walk worthy of all His abundant blessings. (See John 15:7.) Though these wonderful blessings have been made available to us at the cross through His shed blood, yet each promise must be appropriated by our own personal faith, and not that of another; no promise of God is automatically bestowed on us. It must be appropriated by faith.[6]

"Arise, My Soul, Arise"
BY CHARLES WESLEY, 1742

Verse 1
Arise, my soul, arise,
Shake off your guilty fears;
The bleeding sacrifice,
In my behalf appears;
Before the throne my Surety stands,
Before the throne my Surety stands,
My name is written on His hands.

Verse 2
He ever lives above,
For me to intercede;
His all redeeming love,
His precious blood, to plead;
His blood atoned for every race,
His blood atoned for every race,
And sprinkles now the throne of grace.

Verse 3
Five bleeding wounds He bears,
Received on Calvary;
They pour effectual prayers,
They strongly plead for me:
"Forgive him, oh, forgive," they cry,
"Forgive him, oh, forgive," they cry,
"Nor let that ransomed sinner die."

Verse 4

The Father hears Him pray,
His dear Anointed One;
He cannot turn away
The presence of His Son;
The Spirit answers to the blood,
The Spirit answers to the blood,
And tells me I am born of God.

Verse 5

My God is reconciled;
His pardoning voice I hear;
He owns me for His child;
I can no longer fear.
With confidence I now draw nigh,
With confidence I now draw nigh,
And "Father, Abba, Father," cry.

seven

How to Plead
the Blood

At the beginning of the outpouring of the
Holy Spirit in Great Britain around 1908
or 1909, many independent Pentecostal
assemblies sprang up. In these meetings, there
were many evidences of new spiritual life and
power. Since there was no legislative organiza-
tion tying these assemblies together, individual
Christians learned to rely solely on the moving
of the Spirit and His various gifts and operations.
The Holy Spirit began to move in an unusual
way, since there was no council or review board to
enforce any limitations on those Christians.

Many of the believers, so recently baptized
in the Spirit and with the *shekinah* glory resting
upon them, used to plead the blood of Jesus in
strong repetition for all that was burdening their
hearts: unsaved relatives, troubles in the home,
troubles in the nation. Realizing that they had
access to the throne of God, they went in boldly

with the blood of Jesus. Seekers for the baptism in the Holy Spirit were especially helped by doing this. And it was believed by many that the pleading of the blood was a very powerful weapon against evil spirits that would oppose answers to prayer.

DOING BATTLE

"Is this latter point scriptural?" you ask. Well, we must not forget that as soon as Daniel began to pray for the liberation of his people, it took three weeks of "knee battle" while the archangels Michael and Gabriel were battling it out in the heavenlies with the princes of evil. Likewise, today we must often battle with unseen demonic forces before we can get answers to our prayers. The pleading of the blood will cause consternation and confusion to the opposing evil spiritual forces that often delay God's answers. I believe that pleading the blood has a primary place in all intercessory prayer.

Rest assured, when one begins to plead the blood of Jesus out loud, there will be those who will rise up in opposition. Pleading the blood stirs up the backslider and offends the uncrucified flesh of the carnal believer. But in spite of opposition, the use of the blood will clean up any church or prayer group and make way for the operation of the gifts of the Spirit. Oh, the power of the blood of Jesus!

INFUSIONS OF LIFE

Since the life of Jesus is in His blood, if we plead, honor, sprinkle, and sing about it, we are actually introducing the life of the Godhead into our worship. Our prayers and requests become charged with the life and power of Jesus. No wonder Satan will do all he can to suppress practical teaching on the blood. He hates it more than anything else.

Perhaps you have noticed that unbelievers, controlled by evil spirits, often speak the name of Jesus in blasphemy. But have you ever heard a person under the influence of demons blaspheme the blood? Probably not. This is because demons cannot and will not speak of the blood. I have found through practical experience that when people are unable to plead the blood of Jesus audibly, it is a sign that they need strong prayers of deliverance because they are hindered by binding spirits that will not permit them to say "the blood of Jesus."

I would like to especially emphasize the importance of pleading the blood for the baptism in the Spirit. I feel constrained to do this because there are so many different procedures prescribed by so many different groups, yet many hungry seekers have tried all the methods and still haven't received. Isn't it strange that we have all but forgotten that we can receive *nothing* from God apart from His mercy and Jesus' shed blood?

Pastor A. A. Boddy of Sunderland, England, on a return trip from the early Pentecostal outpouring in Norway, said that nowhere in Europe where he had been had he seen people receive the baptism of the Spirit so easily and beautifully as by the pleading of the blood of Jesus. This method was therefore introduced in Boddy's meetings in Parish Hall, and people would even travel across the Atlantic to receive the Pentecostal experience by the pleading of the blood—whereas they had failed to receive the Spirit by other means employed at that time.

GOING TO EXCESS

I realize that many unscriptural methods of receiving the baptism in the Spirit have been introduced by enthusiastic, well-meaning people. Some have suggested that the more noise we make, the more power we will get; others have stressed great fleshly excitement and the thumping of pews, chairs, or even the floor as a means of attracting God's attention. Some have thought that God would be pleased if they deliberately rolled on the floor. These are some of the excesses that have brought great reproach upon the work of the Holy Spirit. We admit, however, that the coming of the Spirit will frequently cause people to drop to the floor "under the power of God," but this is quite different from deliberately throwing oneself to the floor as a means to the baptism! We have been told that the longer one waits, prays, agonizes, and begs for the baptism, the better it is for the supplicant, since it works out something in him that no other spiritual exercise can do. But in so reasoning, aren't we forgetting that the baptism is a free gift?

Baptism in the Holy Spirit is a free gift.

Now, let's examine the scriptural teaching about this matter. Who gives the baptism in the Spirit? None other than Jesus Himself (Matthew 3:11). And where is Jesus? Why, He is in heaven at the Father's right hand (1 Peter 3:22). So, obviously, if we are to receive this free, unmerited gift (Gr. *dwrea*, which means a free, unearned gift or present), we must go to the One who earned it for us and who will give it to all who ask in faith, without any waiting, at any time. If there is any waiting, it is on our part, not on His. Our approach is completely wrong when we think that we have to wait. The Bible teaches us that all believers are now kings and priests (Revelation 1:6) and that we can enter in whenever we desire. There is no waiting list, but we must enter in with His blood.

SIMPLICITY IS BEST

Let me share with you a simple method for receiving the baptism in the Holy Spirit, which I share with seekers everywhere. First of all, it is important for you to relax every muscle in your body. Let all tenseness and uncertainty depart. The baptism in the Holy Spirit is Jesus' work, and there is no reason for you to be tense. Then close your eyes and lift up your hands in adoration and worship; be comfortably seated, and take the precious blood of Jesus on your lips and speak it with your tongue, making it your insistent plea. Be positive and believing in your approach.

Of course, you must do this in simple, reverent faith, having an awe of a holy God who will receive us in the presence of His Son only if we plead His blood. The result of this method of approach is marvelous. Within seconds or minutes, the Holy Spirit begins to answer the pleadings of the blood. Opposing and binding spirits begin to draw back, a way is made between heaven and earth, and soon people become bathed in the glory of God. The most natural thing for them to do at this point is to turn their vocal cords loose and speak in other tongues as the Spirit gives utterance (Acts 2:4).

When the revelation of the pleading of the blood was first given and practiced, there was no teaching on it such as has been given in this book. There was no preaching or exhorta-tion or remarks of any kind on the subject. The practice commenced spontaneously under the strong, compel-ling power of the Holy Spirit. God desired to manifest His power, but it could come forth only as the blood was honored, for His life is in the blood.

Honoring the blood clears the way for the power of God.

So today, honoring and wielding the precious blood of Jesus clears the way for the power of God to be revealed anywhere men and women are press-ing in for the gifts of the Spirit, or for miracles and healings. Receiving the baptism in the Spirit by pleading the blood has been so marvelously easy that some have doubted the result, for there were no fleshly manifestations. It is sometimes forgot-ten that when the Spirit descended on Jesus after He had been baptized in water, He descended in the shape of a dove, quietly, reverently, without outward showiness—and immediately the voice of God was heard. Jesus made no fleshly noises or jerking motions. And that is the way it should be today. The person who goes into the Holy Place pleading the blood will find that God will manifest His *shekinah* glory as He did in the Holy Place of Solomon's temple, and he will commune with God with the voice of other tongues.

Where the blood of Jesus is not honored in this way, and where *"strange fire"* (Leviticus 10:1) is offered instead of the fire that comes in answer to the blood, we have the danger of fanaticism creeping in, with fleshly manifestations that detract from the true moving of the Spirit of God. The Spirit cannot operate on the basis of fleshly offerings, but where the blood of Jesus is offered, then the true move of the Spirit can be expected.

In Romans, we read of Jesus being *"set forth to be a propitiation through faith in his blood, to declare his righteousness for the remission of sins that are past"* (Romans 3:25). We are required to exercise faith in His blood. To plead the blood without faith or with our hearts full of fear is both repulsive and ineffective. When we plead the blood audibly, care should always be taken to do so in simple, believing faith; then it will avail.

ANTIDOTE FOR POISON

A pastor of our acquaintance, who was at one time a naturopathic doctor, once contracted ptomaine poisoning. He placed his hands upon his own body and for twenty minutes pleaded the blood of Jesus, saying, "I plead the blood of Jesus," over and over again. The result of this attack upon Satan's effort to destroy him was that he was completely healed. Others find that the simple repetition of the one word *blood* is sufficient. There are no rules; it is the simple offering of the blood of Jesus in faith, as New Testament priests, that brings results. God will hear the blood-cry and will respect what it has purchased for us. We can obtain all the blessings of the redemption of Christ that we need.

PROPERTY LINES

This truth was brought home to one of my friends, a preaching railroad man from Detroit, Michigan, named Rudy Peterson. Rudy went down to preach in a little mission station in the Bahamas. It had previously been impossible for any missionary to stay and preach because the local natives, whipped up by the devil, used to make terrible noises with tin cans and cries, so as to make worship impossible. When Rudy and a friend of his arrived at the mission station, they walked around the perimeter of the mission, pleading the blood of Jesus out loud. This was done several times, and after that no further trouble was experienced. Rudy, by faith, had put a bloodline right around the chapel.

THE BLOOD AND THE WORD GIFTS

I distinctly remember an amazing instance when pleading the blood enhanced the operation of the word gifts. This most beneficial event started in the most unpropitious circumstances, however. Three of us were seated in a restaurant that had loud jukebox music playing and tobacco smoke filling the air in the place. The conversation turned to the fact that God does reveal causes of troubles through His servants.

Almost immediately, we were approached by a landlady who had an apartment unit that had been empty for eleven months; her employer, the owner of the building, was quite naturally distressed. A word of knowledge was given, followed by a word of wisdom. Within two days, prayer was made in the apartment unit, the devil was rebuked for binding the place, and the blood of Jesus was pleaded out loud in every room and cupboard. A word of prophecy came forth, saying that the apartment would be rented that week, which literally took place. The person concerned was even told the paper in which to advertise the apartment.

Here a combination of three gifts took place to bring about one blessing. The word of knowledge (the reason for the blockage) was given, the word of wisdom (to know what to do to expel the blockage) followed, and a word of prophecy came to foretell that all was well and that the apartment would be rented. All these were gifts brought forth orally, proving them to be the word of God through a human channel. It was not in a church, nor had a season of special prayer preceded the operation of the gifts, but God moved by His Spirit in a prepared sanctified vessel, at the appointed time. Neither was it necessary to get excited, to jump up and down in the restaurant, or to shout and wave arms. The only thing felt was the noxious effects of the tobacco smoke! God wanted His mind brought forth as a word from Him.[7]

PLEADING THE BLOOD BRINGS DELIVERANCE

You can always count on deliverance when you plead the blood.

- The Israelites sprinkled blood in Egypt, and it brought deliverance.
- Rahab used the bloodline token, and it brought deliverance.
- The high priests of the Old Testament sprinkled blood, and it brought forgiveness.
- Jesus sprinkled His own blood and purchased salvation for all mankind!

- We, the New Testament priests serving under our High Priest Jesus, may now sprinkle blood for forgiveness, salvation, redemption, healing, protection, and victory!

Lest anyone should think that the sprinkling of the blood was for the Old Testament saints only, and that the practice ceased when Jesus sprinkled His own precious blood on our behalf, I would remind you of God's command in Exodus 12:24: *"And ye shall observe this thing* [the sprinkling of the blood] *for an ordinance to thee and to thy sons for ever."* If blood must be sprinkled today, then it must be the New Testament priests who do it—and we are those priests if we believe in the Son of God.

eight

The Blood and Divine Health[8]

*My son, attend to my words; incline thine ear
unto my sayings. Let them not depart from thine
eyes; keep them in the midst of thine heart. For
they are life [Gr., zoe] unto those that find them,
and health to all their flesh.*
—Proverbs 4:20–22

Noted in the margin of the King James Version of this Scripture passage is an alternate word for *health:* "medicine." The words, the sayings of God, actually become spiritual medicine for all our flesh. This obviously is intended to cover the whole human body with its bones, brain, nerves, and blood cells. Every single individual cell that carries biological life in it will become further charged with *zoe* life as we allow the Word of God to affect our behavior, and as we become humbly obedient to His commands.

Elsewhere in Proverbs, Solomon wrote that trusting in God and acknowledging His law *"shall be health to thy navel, and marrow to thy bones"* (Proverbs 3:8). Again the alternate word for health is "medicine," and this time the medicine is associated with our navel. I believe the reason for this is that the navel is the part of the body that was at one time connected by the umbilical cord to the mother. The umbilical cord and navel operate as a filtering system to stop impurities from the mother's blood from invading the baby's bloodstream. The navel is the place where life and nourishment enters the body before birth, and it is interesting that this concept is amplified in Psalm 119:130: *"The entrance of thy words giveth light."*

We are the children of God by faith in Jesus Christ, and the church is our womb, or place of safety. However, we have to be fed constantly, and so we have a Holy Spirit umbilical cord that connects us to the source of life, God in heaven. If the navel—the "valve" that controls the inflow of nutrients to the unborn baby—had been diseased before birth, it would not have been able to pass the good food from the mother into the baby's bloodstream, and the infant would have died. As children of God, we must be fed first on the milk of the Word (1 Corinthians 3:2) and then grow to be able to eat the

The Holy Spirit connects us to our source of life—God.

meat of the Word (Hebrews 5:14), and so we will develop into strong, vigorous Christians. Truly the Word of God is health to our navel.

Then we find that this Word is health to the marrow of our bones. This is very interesting, because after birth and after we have ceased to draw life through the umbilical cord, the life process continues in the marrow of the bones. Marrow is the substance in which both the red and white blood corpuscles are manufactured. A balance between the red and white cell levels is maintained, depending on our health. As soon

The Word of God is health to our bones.

as any poisonous or toxic substances invade our bodies, the number of white corpuscles is greatly increased, and these rush to the infected parts and rally round, keeping the poison from further advancing into our bodies.

In Leviticus 17:11, we are given to understand that the life of the body is in the blood, and so the biological life of each of us is contained in strong, vigorous, tiny blood cells. No wonder David said that we are fearfully and wonderfully made (Psalm 139:14); man is God's greatest triumph of creation. Satan can invade the blood cells, and the dread disease of leukemia can take away a life in a few months; but those who take the Word into their beings each day will find that this Word acts as a guard and preventative medicine for these life-maintaining cells. Thus, the very genesis of life in our bones is maintained at one hundred percent fitness and efficiency. Cleansed blood then flows through the body, pumped by a clean heart. The apostle Paul actually used this metaphor concerning the church and God's purpose: *"That he might sanctify and cleanse it with the washing of water by the word"* (Ephesians 5:26).

TAKING A FIRM STAND

Here, then, is a biblical health principle: not that we shouldn't call on the elders for *"the prayer of faith"* (James 5:15)—although this is right and effective—when we are sick, but that there is a deeper way, taking a stand of faith, where we stand firm against all the wiles of the devil and all his fiery darts (Ephesians 6:6, 11). So many of his fiery darts are sicknesses. It is possible to take a stand.

I can testify that I have stood for a quarter of a century by faith in the Word of God for divine health and have found that it works. I have received healing from varicose veins, tobacco, sinus, liver troubles, and the strengthening of my right arm when I tore the bicep muscle. The arm is now as strong as ever, in spite of the fact that the best medical opinion at the time was that I would lose at least 25 percent of the use of that arm.

I believe God is trying to show us today that we can stand in health. Each time Satan tries to attack you in any part of your body, immediately claim the appropriate promise, meditate on it, consume it, and make it a live substance in your bloodstream and in your heart. Since the words and promises of God are *"incorruptible"* seed (1 Peter 1:23), they will sprout up and produce strong plants of promise. If you injest "by His stripes, I am healed" (Isaiah 53:5; 1 Peter 2:24), you will find that the seed

God is trying to show us that we can stand in health.

will produce this in your life, and healing brings health. If you swallow someone's opinion expressed in doubt—possibly telling you of some loved one who died with the same symptoms—then doubt has been sown. Doubt is not the incorruptible seed of the Word of God, and so the seed of doubt will produce its inevitable plant of sickness and death. What you sow, you reap (Galatians 6:7)!

Keep ingesting the promises of God. Keep sowing seeds of God because *"as* [a man] *thinketh in his heart, so is he"* (Proverbs 23:7). The heart pumps the life-giving blood to every part of the flesh of a person. If the blood is pure, every other tissue will be pure. If we fill our minds with filth by reading salacious literature, by attending X-rated movies, and by listening to filthy stories, then inevitably we will produce the fruits of this sowing:

> *For from within, out of the heart of men, proceed evil thoughts, adulteries, fornications, murders, thefts, covetousness, wickedness, deceit, lasciviousness, an evil eye, blasphemy, pride, foolishness: all these evil things come from within, and defile the man.* (Mark 7:21–23)

If any of these things trouble you in your life, you have not been fully cleansed within, and so your mind and body will show the effects of this internal filth. The true mind is in the heart, for *"with the heart man believeth unto righteousness"* (Romans 10:10). Once the mind has been cleansed, then it can be said of us that we have *"the mind of Christ"* (1 Corinthians 2:16; see also Philippians 2:5). Christ's mind was pure, and He was never sick. He did not suffer because of His own sicknesses; He suffered for our sicknesses, so that through His death we might be healed and find life and health.

CLEANSING, HEALING WORDS

Wise King Solomon wrote, *"There is that speaketh like the piercings of a sword: but the tongue of the wise is health"* (Proverbs 12:18). The words that proceed from our tongues will give clear evidence of the state of our health. Dr. William Standish Reed, M.D., of the Christian Medical Foundation, Medford, Oregon, informed us that such terribly destructive things as criticism, grumbling, self-pity, hatred, cursing, and bearing grudges are the cause of much physical sickness, and all these things are manifest through the tongue. Solomon again wrote, *"Thou art snared with the words of thy mouth, thou art taken with the words of thy mouth"* (Proverbs 6:2). It is we ourselves who destroy ourselves. Satan puts into our hearts all these evil thoughts, which find their almost inevitable expression as words in our mouths. As we speak

We can fight Satan's attacks with the sword of the Spirit.

them, we ensnare ourselves so that Satan has the perfect right to come along and tell us there is no hope for us, for He is the angel of death, and the wages of sin is death.

No wonder Solomon warned that negative words, such as those of hate, envy, and criticism, are as *"piercings of a sword."* There is always a positive for a negative, a day for a night, light for darkness. Thank God, there is another sword than that of Satan—the sword of the Spirit, which is the Word of God. The same tongue that spewed out vile, evil things that corrupted and destroyed us can be tamed, not by ourselves, but only by a true work of the Spirit of God in transforming our spirits. Our whole nature is changed, and now the heart that was the cesspool of every foul thought becomes cleansed by the blood of Jesus. Instead of unclean water spilling out of our mouths, now the Holy Spirit will give us words of truth, of life, and of health. *The tongue of the wise is health.*

COMMUNION AND HEALTH

To approach any servant of God who has a healing ministry for the prayer of faith is useless unless we first examine our hearts to see whether there is any wicked way in us. It is not enough to have entered into the covenant of salvation and to agree that Jesus is the Great Physician, unless we first examine ourselves, which we are supposed to do every time we approach the communion table. We can always appropriate divine health afresh around the communion table. It is the table of the Lord spread before us in the presence of our enemies. It is loaded down with good things (Psalm 23:5). The apostle Paul was insistent when he wrote, *Let a man examine himself, and so let him eat of that bread, and drink of that cup* (1 Corinthians 11:28). As we partake of the bread, we are actually partaking by faith of the very health that was in the body of Jesus, which was broken for us. As we drink the wine, we are receiving by faith the very life that was in Jesus, for the life—His life—is in His blood (Leviticus 17:11).

The apostle John made it equally clear that we are only cleansed from all sin by the blood of Jesus as we continue to walk in the light of His Word and obey it (1 John 1:7). If we grumble, criticize, or bear grudges with an unforgiving spirit, we put ourselves outside the terms of the new covenant in Christ's blood. Under those conditions, it won't matter how many people pray for us or how many times we are prayed for; we will not receive our healing until the sin of these things is confessed and put under the blood! Once these terrible, destroying sins are confessed and forsaken, it must be a permanent act of forsaking, and we must always be on guard against the subtle temptations of Satan to cause us again to use our tongues in this soul-destroying manner. You must *"work out your own salvation with fear and trembling"* (Philippians 2:12), not treat it as some light, inconsequential thing.

nine

The Application of the Blood

One dark night many years ago, I went out to my garage to get the car. There was no light in the garage, and I forgot that someone had partially driven a nail into one of the walls. As I walked hastily to the car, my forehead was grazed by the protruding nail. I pulled my head away quickly, realizing what had happened, but it was too late—there was a nasty wound on my head. Immediately I began to plead the blood of Jesus. In half an hour, there wasn't a mark on my head! So, you see, pleading the blood is a very practical thing.

Most of the questions directed to me regarding this matter have to do with how to apply the blood of Jesus in practical form to any situation that may be controlled by Satan. The crucial question is one of practical usage rather than the theological concept. Theology teaches that Jesus shed His blood once for the sins of the world, and that is all there is to say about it! The danger lies in allowing this to become a historical, lifeless fact rather than a present, potent reality.

DISINFECTING WOUNDS

So let's talk about how to apply the blood. In the natural world, we would have no difficulty understanding how to apply disinfectant to an infection. We would take the disinfectant and sprinkle or pour it on the infection, and the result would be that all germs and living organisms present in that infection would die.

Now, we should have no difficulty in doing the same thing spiritually. Wherever Satan is at work, we must apply the only corrective antidote there is—the blood of Jesus. There is absolutely no alternative, no substitute. Prayer, praise, worship, and devotion all have their part in our approach to God, but the blood of Jesus is the only effective counteragent to corruption.

This is why Satan has always tried to take the blood out of our churches. If there is no disinfectant, then his demons are free to continue their deadly work of destruction in spirit, soul, and body.

Having concluded that the blood of Jesus is our only remedy, how are we to obtain it and use it? In the Old Testament, the head of each household took a bunch of hyssop, dipped it into the blood, and sprinkled or daubed it on the lintels and doorposts of the houses of the Israelites. But in the spiritual realm, we take the blood by faith and then speak it, which is really a form of intercessory prayer. Each time we plead the blood, we are offering the only plea that can bring any results in intercession.

Think of it this way. The word *blood,* spoken in faith once, could be likened to one drop of blood splashed upon the evil, corruptive situation with which we have to deal in prayer. Obviously, no one putting disinfectant upon corruption at the bottom of a garbage container would use only one drop, would they? So the more we plead the blood, the more power we are bringing to bear against this evil situation.

However, let me warn against rote repetition. Obviously, pleading the blood mechanically in vain repetition is ineffective and foolish, especially to the unbeliever. But for the child of God who pleads the blood in faith, it quickly brings wonderful results. The whole approach is so simple and obvious to the spiritual mind that we are often amazed that so many people miss it.

PHYSICAL AND SPIRITUAL SACRIFICES

In Old Testament times, the priests offered physical sacrifices of animals. The flesh was burned with fire, but the blood was drained into basins and was used by being sprinkled. In New Testament times, we are priests who *"offer up spiritual sacrifices, acceptable to God by Jesus Christ"* (1 Peter 2:5). Spiritual sacrifices are the New Testament counterparts of the Old Testament physical sacrifices. As New Testament believer-priests, we are to take the living blood of Jesus and "sprinkle" it before the Lord by repeating the word *blood*. Immediately, we begin to bring Satan's work into captivity and nullify his evil workings.

The blood of Abel spoke vengeance, but the blood of Jesus speaks peace, pardon, and reconciliation for all who are bound by Satan. As we speak the word *blood,* we must remember that the blood of Jesus carries all the power, Spirit, and life that is in Jesus. As the blood of a human carries his life, so does the blood of Jesus carry the life of the Son of God. Each time we say the word *blood* in faith, we are bringing the creative life force of the universe to bear upon the destroying power of Satan.

How Often Is Necessary?

I do not mean to suggest for a moment that the blood does not avail for you at all times, and that therefore you must continually plead the blood to keep yourself covered. I remember a young man who approached my wife after one of my teaching sessions and said in grave earnestness, "Sister Whyte, how often do you think we should plead the blood? Should we, for instance, plead it every half hour?"

Mrs. Whyte said later with some amusement that she could just see him standing there with a stopwatch, saying, "Well, now, I must plead the blood!" Of course, such an idea is ridiculous. No, the point I am trying to make is that in every situation where you sense that you are under the attack of Satan or needing special protection, that is the time to plead the blood. By so doing, you are reminding God that you are trusting in His mercy, you are reminding Satan that he cannot touch you as long as you are under the blood, and you are reminding yourself of the ground of your confidence in Christ.

VALIDATION OF TONGUES

Pleading the blood is also a good way to test the validity of many spiritual manifestations. We are frequently asked the question, "If Satan can speak through us in tongues, how can I know that my tongue is of God?" This is an important and valid question. I have already said that a person who is bound in some area by Satan will find it difficult or impossible to plead the blood. If a person speaks in a demonic tongue, he will not be able to plead the blood. So this is a good way to test the reality of your tongues-speaking experience.

To receive the baptism in the Holy Spirit with the evidence of tongues, I always teach seekers to plead the blood out loud in faith. They might start haltingly, but as the Spirit of God descends upon them, and the inner cleansing begins to take effect, they find that their tongues are beginning to enjoy this practice in faith, and the word *blood* begins to tumble out of their mouths in great boldness.

Seekers usually receive such an anointing of the Spirit in answer to the cry of the blood that words of an unknown tongue begin to be manifested and a torrent of *glossolalia* flows. In this case, there can be no doubt whatsoever that the tongues spoken are truly a manifestation of the Holy Spirit.

ABANDONING SELF-WILL

Some, however, are far more hesitant and find it difficult to abandon their wills to God; they are uncertain, fearful, and cautious in their approach to Him. On the other hand, they may have been taught that they already had the fullness of the

Spirit when they were converted; this teaching can be a stumbling block to many.

We must always bear in mind that speaking in tongues is an evidence of overflow, not of static fullness. We can become confused about these two distinct experiences. John the Baptist was full of the Holy Spirit before Pentecost, and he would have overflowed in the upper room had he been there. Similarly, since Mary was in the upper room, she did overflow, and out of her mouth came a torrent of worship in unknown tongues.

BANISH YOUR FEARS

Hesitant people who are full of fears and doubts are a little more difficult to help, but experience has shown that great progress can be made if we can just get them to begin pleading the blood. They usually begin very quietly, though, almost in a whisper, and we have to encourage them to go on with more determination and holy abandon.

As they do so, they gradually begin to disperse their fears, and new words begin to be spoken, sometimes haltingly, mixed in with pleading the blood. Sometimes they will revert to saying, "I can't," which is an expression of the spirit of fear stirred up by the pleading of the blood. Nevertheless, they are urged to start pleading the blood again. It usually becomes easier as doubts and fears are driven out, and soon they begin to speak in other tongues, often to their astonishment and joy.

It will be readily seen that this method of receiving the baptism in the Spirit is very effective. In fact, in my many years of ministry, I have rarely seen it fail. Many chronic seekers who have not been able to receive the baptism in the Spirit by other means have quickly "come through" by pleading the blood. When people have asked for the baptism in the Holy Spirit in prayer lines in many countries of the world, I have simply instructed them to start repeating the word *blood,* and within a matter of seconds they have begun to speak in tongues. Usually I then call over another worker and suggest that he or she praise God with those who are being baptized so that they do not stop speaking in tongues. They are now entering another spiritual dimension, and it is wonderfully strange! It is important that they do not begin to doubt at this point. I then go on to the next one in line and begin all over again.

Pleading the blood disperses fear and doubt.

Where there are many to receive the baptism in the Spirit, I find it most effective to teach them a little about the significance of pleading the blood of Jesus. When we actually begin to plead the blood, we often have twenty or more seekers pleading together. Very soon, one by one, the Spirit enters fully into them and they overflow in tongues. The blood of Jesus has great power when spoken in faith!

CONTINUAL CLEANSING FROM SPIRITUAL POISON

The inward sign for all Christians is the impervious power of the blood of Jesus that has cleansed us, and will continually cleanse us, from all sin and temptations to sin. Under the law of God, a symbol was given all who were ordained into the Levitical priesthood. Blood of the consecration sacrifice was put upon the tip of Aaron's right ear (Leviticus 8:23–24) and elsewhere, and then on the tips of the ears of his sons. When the crown of thorns was jammed onto Jesus' head, His own blood spurted and ran down over His ears, and fell to the ground. All who come to the cross today may have His blood applied to their ears by faith. The continual presence of the blood upon our ears will actually destroy all poison assailing our hearing and nullify it completely, neutralizing its deadly effects upon our spirits and minds, so that our minds remain uncontaminated.

This built-in cleansing operates continually, providing that we daily confess our sins and depart from them as something loathsome. The power of the blood of Jesus is ineffective if we tempt God by deliberately listening to gossip or filth or go to places where evil things take place to be entertained by them. *"Let no man say when he is tempted, I am tempted of God....But every man is tempted, when he is drawn away of his own lust, and enticed"* (James 1:13–14). We cannot blame God for our backsliding, but only ourselves, for it is then that Satan takes advantage through his demon spirits to inject spiritual poison into us. It will then be necessary for complete repentance and turning away in abhorrence, so that the blood of Jesus will neutralize this deadly poison.

Pleading the blood cleanses our lives.

The Old Testament application of this principle occurred when the three Hebrew youths were cast into the fiery furnace and not burned, and when Daniel was cast into the den of lions and not harmed. In both cases, the power of the Spirit was stronger than the power of Satan. This is why John equated the blood of Jesus with the Spirit of God. (See 1 John 5:8.) Wherever the blood of Jesus is used in application to the ears, heart, thumbs, or toes, we are assured of the protection of the omnipresent Spirit of God, for the "Spirit answers to the blood," as the old Wesleyan hymn says.

In Leviticus 8:30, it is evident that the blood was applied as well as the oil: *"And Moses took of the anointing oil* [typifying the Holy Spirit], *and of the blood* [typifying the blood of Jesus] *which was upon the altar* [typifying the cross], *and sprinkled it upon Aaron,...and upon his sons."* Jesus did the sprinkling upon the cross, and we may avail ourselves of that sprinkled blood today by applying it to ourselves. As the writer of Hebrews put it, *"Having our hearts sprinkled from an evil conscience"* (Hebrews 10:22). When we plead the blood of Jesus, we attract the power of the Holy Spirit.

As the heart is the center of operations of our spiritual life, which likewise affects our whole triune person, we find that an inbuilt spiritual cleansing is continually in operation, even while we sleep. What comes into our ears or eyes or mouth is killed, just as certain insecticides sprinkled on the doorsteps of our homes destroy roaches and ants before they penetrate our dwellings.[9]

PRACTICAL APPLICATIONS

When the children were small, we often had to plead the blood over their scratches and scrapes!

One day in particular when little Stephen was in the kitchen with my wife, he got badly burned. It was a cold day, and we had opened the oven to help circulate a little extra heat through the house. Stephen accidentally backed into the oven lid, which was quite hot, and got a bad burn across the back of his legs. Instantly, Olive and I began pleading the blood.

"It will be all right," I said. "The blood has never lost its power!"

That night when we were going to bed, I said, "By the way, Stephen, how are your legs?"

Olive and I looked, and there wasn't the faintest trace of a burn.

The Word of God teaches, *"When I see the blood, I will pass over you, and the plague shall not be upon you to destroy you"* (Exodus 12:13). Paul told us that Jesus is our Passover (1 Corinthians 5:7). He became our Passover by shedding His own precious blood. There is nothing more precious to believers than this!

Holy Spirit Baptism and the Blood[10]

Many ways have been taught whereby believers might receive the baptism in the Spirit, some sensible and scriptural, but others more emotional and not so scriptural! Right now, I want to show you how you can receive this baptism by pleading or sprinkling the blood of Jesus. I have literally seen hundreds of people quickly receive this gift by following these simple and scriptural teachings.

IT'S A GIFT TO RECEIVE, NOT TO EARN

First, we need to bear in mind that the apostles called the baptism in the Spirit *"the gift of the Holy Ghost"* (Acts 2:38; 10:45). The Greek word *dwrea* means a free gift—that is to say, it cannot be earned or merited, but can only be gladly accepted. John explained that it was Jesus alone who was appointed by the Father to give us this gift, and so we must go to Him and graciously take it out of His hand. This is where so many make a big mistake; they believe that if they act in a religious manner, suffer through some religious exercise like fasting, or begin to feel emotional, then Jesus will force this gift on them and make them speak in tongues. I have often heard misguided people say, "If God wants me to receive the Holy Spirit, He will give it to me." They never seem to realize that giving is a two-way experience; it is both giving and receiving. He gives; we take. If we do not take, we do not receive. In other words, if we do not cooperate with Him, we receive nothing, however pious we think we are. The Holy Spirit is not given on the grounds of our worthiness or denomination or piousness, but solely on the basis of our personal faith (Galatians 3:2–5).

All gifts of God are two-way. He gives; we receive.

Some have taught that the Holy Spirit only comes into a holy vessel, which is true if we mean imputed holiness, but certainly not if we mean "worked up" holiness. These people have the idea that long waiting or tarrying is necessary to receive this gift, and they feel they earn merit points because of the time they spend praying, begging, groaning, agonizing, and sometimes rolling. As long as we insist on trying to earn the gift of the Holy Spirit, God will let us wait! We are not beggars, but sons and daughters. All gifts of God—whether salvation, healing, or the baptism in the Spirit—may and should be received and utilized as soon as we take them in faith.

To Tarry or Not to Tarry

I remember holding a combined meeting with a Pentecostal pastor in Toronto some years ago. I had taken about six of his members and prayed all of them through to the baptism by pleading the blood of Jesus. Yet their pastor stated they had had a forced baptism and that if they did speak in tongues, they had done so "in the flesh" because they had been pressured into it. This became another cliché: that one could speak in tongues in the flesh as well as in the Spirit, and that it was necessary to tarry for the coming or anointing of the Spirit for a person to speak in tongues.

This position, of course, ignores the obvious truth, as found in 1 John 2:27, that the anointing of the Spirit abides within us and that the Holy Spirit will teach us all things. Obviously, if the Holy Spirit dwells within us as a welcome visitor, we do not have to wait for Him to arrive when He is already inside! Thus, a Spirit-filled person may at any time start praising in tongues, which is a most edifying experience that was strongly recommended and practiced by Paul. (See 1 Corinthians 14:2–4, 14–18.)

Today there is no purpose in tarrying after a Pentecostal encounter. All we have to do is reach out in our human spirit and receive His Spirit, and as soon as we cooperate with Him and speak the words He gives us, we will experience the outflowing of the *glossolalia,* or other tongues. If we refuse to speak forth and tarry for years, it will be our fault

We must reach out in faith and accept God's gift.

and not God's. Far from producing progressive sanctification, the long-term tarrying in some cases has produced such defeat and despair that many have given up seeking altogether. Meanwhile, they kept their mouths shut tight as they were waiting for God to do everything!

Again, this matter of God filling man to overflowing is mutual cooperation between man and God. Don't we find this same excuse in many who desire healing? They say, "If God wants me to be healed, He will heal me." Not so! We must reach out in faith, receive His healing, and join it to ourselves. Likewise, those who seek hungrily to be baptized in the Spirit must take and receive Him. The power will be manifested through us only as we turn on the faucet of our tongues and speak. This principle applies equally to the gifts of interpretation and prophecy.

Fortunately, in this present charismatic outpouring, the teaching of tarrying is relatively unknown. Thousands are receiving the baptism the moment that hands are laid upon them, and they use their lips and tongues to speak forth the praises of God. As you are reading, if you just start pleading the precious blood of Jesus as your prayer, do not be surprised if you begin speaking in tongues as the Spirit gives you the utterance (Acts 2:4).

HEAVENLY PROTOCOL

There is a divine protocol. In the same way that a warrior would appear before a king to receive a medal, we must appear in the presence of the Son of God to receive this gift. To appear before Jesus in heaven is a breathtakingly awesome thought! To go into the throne room of glory requires that we approach Him in the right way as He sits on His throne. What is this way? It is the way of the blood. When the high priest went into the Holy of Holies in the Old Testament tabernacle, he went in with the blood of a sacrifice and sprinkled it upon the mercy seat. The Holy Place represented heaven, the dwelling place of God, and the mercy seat typified His Son, since Jesus is our resting place at the end of our journey of sin, and He sprinkled Himself in His own blood. As we come to the mercy seat, we embrace the blood shed for us.

When the outpouring of the Spirit occurred at the beginning of the twentieth century, especially in the British Isles, a new revelation of the blood of Jesus was given to many. It was quickly realized by these early Pentecostal pioneers that God honored the prayer of the blood. The practice of "pleading the blood" came into sharp focus, and those who sought the Holy Spirit baptism by the pleading or honoring of the blood of Jesus quickly received deeper, dimensional baptisms. Some actually saw rivers of blood in visions as they used this word in prayer. Visions were given and prophecies heard that magnified the blood of Jesus.

> *The blood is the price paid for every redemptive blessing.*

What did this revelation mean? We know that Scripture teaches we are *"bought with a price"* (1 Corinthians 6:20; 7:23), and this means that we are no longer our own. We belong to Jesus, and the purchase price of our redemption was paid in the blood of Jesus, which contained His life. A simple analogy will help us to understand. If we go into a store to buy an item costing one dollar and we offer that dollar to the cashier, we will be given the article without question. We will not try to convince the store manager of our worthiness to have the article or to impress him by our well-articulated arguments. We simply pay the money and receive the article we want. Now, what is the price paid for every redemptive blessing? Obviously, the blood of Jesus. So it is not necessary to make long prayers, to beat the pews, to shout to heaven, or to roll on the floor to attract the attention of the One who gives us the gift of the Holy Spirit. Note, the baptism in the Holy Spirit is a gift and thus free to us because He purchased it with His own blood.

The analogy breaks down a bit here because we do not offer anything for this gift; instead, we honor the price that Jesus paid. Remember, even though the glorious gift of the Holy Spirit is free to us, there was still a price paid for the blessing. All we have to do is to go into the presence of Jesus in heaven and simply say, "Lord, we plead Your blood; we honor Your blood." God knows that there is no other One who can give us this gift but His Son, and He knows that because He promised, He gives it to all who seek Him in faith, honoring the price. He has absolutely no other option than to give us this remarkable gift. As soon as we receive it, we will use it and manifest tongues!

The blood is also the price paid for our redemption, for we are *"bought with a price"* (1 Corinthians 6:20; 7:23). Thus, the blood of Jesus is the only recognized currency in heaven, the Holy Place of God. Remember that although the Holy Spirit is freely given to us, this precious gift had to be purchased for us at the great price of the shed blood of Jesus. Someone had to pay the price. Therefore, we approach Jesus in the throne room of heaven by first worshipping Him in our spirits, quietly and reverently. We then take His precious blood by faith and begin to sprinkle drops of it in His presence, thereby demonstrating that our entire faith is centered in the blood and not in ourselves or our self-righteousness or our denomination or our race or our education! Our faith is only in the blood.

Each time we say the word *blood* audibly, it is like sprinkling one drop. As we say it several times by repetition, we offer several drops. Try to empty your mind of other thoughts and concentrate on the sacrifice of Calvary and the blood that was shed on the cross. If you offer it freely by sprinkling or repetition, Jesus will answer you, and you will quickly feel the Holy Spirit immersing your whole being. At this point, surrender your tongue, take words from the Holy Spirit, and begin to praise God in an unknown tongue. You need to be relaxed and in a spirit of worship. If you are tense, relax and sit down, just as the disciples were all seated on the day of Pentecost in the upper room (Acts 2:1–2).

In the initial Pentecost experience of those gathered in the upper room, it is recorded that *"**they** were all filled with the Holy Ghost, and*

began to speak *with other tongues, as the Spirit gave them utterance"* (Acts 2:4, emphasis added). So many have the entirely mistaken idea that the Holy Spirit began to speak! This was a matter of mutual cooperation. As in water baptism, the candidate relaxes and trusts the minister to bury him under the water, so we must relax and trust the Holy Spirit to come into us and give us the words that we alone must speak. If we do not speak, His words cannot be heard, and there can be no outflow

If we do not speak, the Spirit's words cannot be heard.

of the Spirit. Our tongues in fact become a kind of faucet that we turn on to allow the river of life to flow! *"They…began to speak…as the Spirit gave them utterance."*

The Holy Spirit is a guest. He will not make you do anything. If you wish to speak His divine words, whether in tongues or prophecy or some other charismatic utterance, you will use your own faith and begin to speak. As the words of God begin to flow out of you, bypassing your mind, you will hear the mind of God spoken, just as others within the sound of your voice will.

The pleading of the blood accomplishes something else, too. As soon as you make up your mind to approach Jesus Christ for the gift of the Holy Spirit, Satan will send his demonic forces to stop you from receiving. He will try to come between you and the Giver. The audible pleading or sprinkling of the blood of Jesus by repetition drives him and his hellish hosts back, and they flee in alarm, which is why many have experienced a sudden immersion into the Holy Spirit and come up praising God in a loud voice in tongues. The blood speaks to God for mercy, pardon, and grace, but to Satan it speaks defeat, scattering, and consternation.

We need to remember that some Christians who come to receive the baptism are still bound in certain areas of their lives by evil things from Satan. Evil habits and thoughts still plague many children of God. Such usually fail to receive their personal Pentecost by some of the better-known methods of seeking the Spirit. So little has been understood about the ministry of deliverance that bound Christians have worshipped in full gospel churches for years until they finally became so discouraged that they ceased seeking the gift of the Holy Spirit. This should not be. Pleading the blood will reveal the binding spirits, and they can then be dealt with and cast out by the person praying with the seeker. Some seekers will dislike the pleading of the blood and consider it foolish or repulsive, but as they are encouraged, they may even find it very difficult, if not impossible, to repeat the word *blood*. Only the prayer of faith in deliverance will deliver such people to make them ready and open for the infilling of the Spirit of God. Fear is one of these binding spirits, quite apart from bad habits and thoughts.

FALSE BAPTISMS

Mention should also be made of spurious baptisms in the Spirit. People can be possessed of an evil spirit for years and be bound. Such a person may seek for the infilling of the Holy Spirit but will be unable to receive because *"other spirits"* (Matthew 12:45) insist on taking over, especially in praise services. These are often religious spirits that simulate the things of God. Instead of the Holy Spirit coming in and giving words for the joyous candidate to praise God with, the evil spirit already within will start to speak in another language, but the look on the person's face will usually be far from restful and peaceful and joyous; it will be demonic and tense, and the voice probably hysterical. Furthermore, the life of the person after such an experience will not show the fruits of the Spirit, which helps to explain some of the strange baptisms that we have seen and heard about in our churches. If the seeker will begin by pleading the blood of Jesus in faith when approaching the mercy seat, these alien spirits will have to declare themselves and be cast out, thus delivering the individual.

This shocking exposé of the subtle workings of Satan should not alarm us. The Bible is full of cases of demons crying out and using words that were well understood, such as *"Let us alone....art thou come to destroy us? I know thee who thou art, the Holy One of God"* (Mark 1:24). Such happenings are tolerable when we read about them in the Bible, but when they spring out from the pages and into our churches today, we become afraid. If the Holy Spirit can give us the ability to *"speak with the tongues of men and of angels"* (1 Corinthians 13:1), couldn't evil spirits also speak through us in known tongues as well as unknown tongues? The blood is the only safeguard we have. It is enough. Satan cannot penetrate the blood of Jesus, but he does run when we sing, shout, and plead the blood!

HONORING THE BLOOD

The very moment we start honoring and pleading the blood, there is an instant reaction in heaven. God is honor-bound to give us the blessing because we are once again taking Jesus' precious blood in faith and honoring or sprinkling it, as the priests did with the blood of sacrifices in Old Testament times; but now, as New Testament priests, we are offering to God the spiritual sacrifice of the blood (1 Peter 2:5). We don't offer literal blood as the priests did in Old Testament times, but we now offer or sprinkle the blood of Jesus spiritually.

In the early days of the outpouring of the Spirit, the earnest and hungry people simply went before the Lord seeking His gift. They relaxed, and many cupped their hands as if they were making an offering, which they were, but it was a spiritual offering. As the priests of old sprinkled many drops of blood, so can we as New Testament priests sprinkle many drops of blood spiritually.

Each time we repeat the word *blood* with our lips, it is a prayer and an act of faith. We are only offering His precious blood, the price paid for this redemptive blessing. The effect of this prayer approach is astonishing. The Holy Spirit will descend upon us almost at once, and then we will find it difficult to say the word *blood* anymore. Something strange will begin to happen to our jaws and our tongues, and at this point we give place to the Spirit and take the words He gives us, and they start to flow through us as we deliberately stop saying the word *blood* and just speak forth the words of the Spirit. As we start, it is like opening a water valve or faucet, and then the living water begins to flow forth from our lips and tongues. We are now speaking in other tongues as the Spirit gives us utterance.

SPEAK UP

It is very important that we understand that it is *we* who do the speaking. Let us refer to Acts 2:4 where we read that it was the disciples who *"began to speak."* If they had refused to cooperate and turn on the valve, there would have been no flow of living water! Some wait for God to start speaking, and so they refuse to pray and they keep their mouths shut! Others go on beseeching in English or whatever their native tongue may be. They beg for what rightly belongs to them. It is the gift of the Holy Spirit. Some old-fashioned seeking meetings were painful, and many prayed and prayed for years but never received. Had they known how to honor the blood of Jesus, they would have received.

The late Smith Wigglesworth used to say that in prophesying or interpreting, the first few words are from our own minds, and then, as we begin to speak, the Spirit takes over and the flow is of God. Our initial approach to God, therefore, must be to open our mouths and speak. However, it is sufficient that we simply honor the blood. Then, as the Spirit begins to give us the supernatural words, we keep on speaking—we must not stop—and we will hear ourselves speaking in other tongues as the Spirit gives us the utterance.

Many make the mistake of thinking that they are going to hear the words in their minds before they speak them forth. This is not so, for the Holy Spirit flows only through our human spirits, never our minds, actually bypassing our minds. When we begin to speak in new tongues, we will hear ourselves and the strange words in the same manner as others hear them. It is the same with prophecy. We do not know what we are going to speak forth; we will hear as others do, and we all get blessed.

I well remember a lady who came to our church in about 1950. She was sent to me by a relative, who had told her that I would pray for her to receive the Holy Spirit. She was told absolutely nothing about what would happen. All that had been explained to her was that this was a great experience to have; so the lady came before me. I simply asked her to plead or repeat the word *blood*, which she did quite obediently. Almost immediately she burst forth, praising God in a new language, and then she stopped and looked at me with astonishment and said, "What was that?" It was a little amusing, but I encouraged her to continue, which she immediately did with tears of joy running down her face. Later, explanations from the Bible were given to her.

Wherever I have been privileged to minister in many countries of the world, I have taught this method of seeking God's gift of the baptism of the Holy Spirit. Almost one hundred percent of those who have come have begun to speak in tongues as they were encouraged. Some who come are full of discouragement and doubts, for they have approached God with a lack of understanding. They have prayed in English. They have gotten tense and shouted. They have begged and implored and besought Jesus—and nothing has happened. They did not understand that it is impossible to speak in English with the mind and to speak in tongues by the Spirit at the same time. The mind must get out of the way and give precedence to our human spirit. Like goes with like—the Spirit of God merges with our human spirits.

OVERCOMING DIFFICULTIES

Others come to us who are not completely dedicated to the Lord. They are following from afar, but they want the blessings. They are probably bound by some habit, or they have an unforgiving spirit or a critical attitude toward people. They may have been immersed in some form of the occult, such as horoscopes, spiritism, or Ouija boards, and they have attracted to themselves unclean spirits. These spirits will react quickly to the pleading of the blood, which will cleanse them out of their hiding places. Often, deliverances begin to take place among these people when they plead the blood of Jesus, and they will start choking or coughing as the spirits are ejected because of the cry of the blood. As they press on, the deliverance takes place, and then the coughing is replaced by halting tongues, which gradually increase in volume and clarity. Sometimes the person being delivered will speak in tongues, then cough, then speak in tongues, then cough, until the channel is clear and the tongues are clear. In such cases, it is obvious that the seeker actually helps to clean himself up by using the blood as a purifier.

Many, in times past, have never been able to receive the baptism of the Spirit because they have been bound and have not known the way to get free, and their pastors have not known either. It has been strictly a hit-or-miss affair, and despondency has descended upon those who are bound. But the use of the blood will disclose lurking spirits that Satan had put there to resist the incoming of the Spirit! I have been able to help so many of these chronic seekers, because they first needed a measure of deliverance before the Spirit could enter them.

Many reading about this method have applied the instructions. I received a letter from a man conducting a Bible class in Nigeria, West Africa. His students were all evangelical and none had received the baptism of the Spirit. He instructed them to start pleading the blood, and within a very short time twenty Nigerians were praising God in tongues. All he had done was to read and act on some of my early writings on the subject. I pray that thousands will seek God's blessing of the baptism of the Holy Spirit by approaching the mercy seat in heaven, where Jesus is. He will respond and fill you quickly with the Spirit.

NEW DIMENSIONS

This glorious experience can be appreciated only *after* you receive. The gift brings you into an entirely new dimension of power with God. It does not alter your status as a child of God, for Jesus was still the Son of God before He was anointed by the Spirit in the Jordan River. We waste our time with those who oppose us if we try to argue them into this blessing, for they must thirst first. If our friends are not thirsty, the baptism is not for them.

It is beautiful to see many today as they first begin to speak in tongues. Their faces light up, a new look of glory appears on them, they walk with a lighter step, and praises begin to be heard from their lips. "Hallelujah" and "Praise the Lord" become the norm, much to the embarrassment of some of their dry Christian friends!

eleven

Protection through the Blood

As I have explained earlier, the word *atonement* means "a covering." We as believers can be protected with an impervious covering that keeps us safe from the enemy.

THE KEEPING POWER OF THE BLOOD

This is why the apostle John taught us that *"the wicked one toucheth* [the believer] *not"* (1 John 5:18). The qualification for this state of protection, however, is that *"he that is begotten of God keepeth himself"* (verse 18). This basically means that believers must keep themselves consciously and consistently under the blood. Unconfessed sin is never under the blood; only when it is confessed and forsaken are we covered and protected.

I have received letters from many parts of the world telling of spectacular deliverances taking place when people have audibly pleaded the blood after reading an earlier edition of this book. Of course, not only do we actually plead the blood against the devil and his demons, but we also command Satan to loose his grip in the name of Jesus. The actual pleading of the blood must generally be used in conjunction with the command given in the name of Jesus. This is especially important when we are ministering to others. We need to plead the blood to keep ourselves safe from any satanic kickback while the sufferer is being released from his terrible bondage.

Testimony after testimony can be given by those who dare to oppose Satan in his dealings with humanity and minister to others through the power of the blood. My experience shows, however, that even many Christians are cruelly bound and oppressed by demons; in fact, it is Christians who are seeking deliverance today far more than unbelievers.

PROTECTION ON THE ROAD

In the winter of 1971, I had taken a party of fourteen young people to skate on Lake Simcoe, Ontario. I was driving a station wagon that had almost bald front tires. On our return on an icy road, the front of the vehicle went out of control and ran into a snow bank. As it left the road, I pleaded the blood out loud, and the car came to rest in a snowbank about eighteen inches from a telephone pole. One can imagine what might have happened had we hit the pole head-on. The blood saved us! Soon we were dragged out by a tow truck, and we proceeded on our way, rejoicing.

Unknown to us, my wife was ahead of us on Highway 400, which was also ice covered. Suddenly, her car also went completely out of control, spinning in a circle. My wife pleaded the blood out loud, and the car came to rest facing the other way against a snowbank. On the other side of this bank was a twenty-foot drop! Once again, she was saved by the blood. Satan had made a determined attack upon us both, but we opposed him by wielding the blood of Jesus.

SECURITY CHECKS

A more unusual testimony comes from Reverend W. G. of Phoenix, Arizona. He decided one day to sprinkle the blood of Jesus over his paycheck; within a short time he received an increase in salary! One of the Christian ladies known to him then did the same thing and received an unexpected bonus in cash. I know that such testimonies are scorned by carnal-minded Christians. However, carnal Christians will never enter into any fight against Satan's bindings, much less in the matter of salary and possessions!

Always be quick to plead the blood when you realize that Satan is attacking you, either physically or emotionally. Blue Mondays turn into days of rejoicing for those who cover themselves with the blood. But you must use it; you must sprinkle it by faith.

PROTECTION FROM MUGGERS

A lady who originally worshipped in our church before she went to work as a nurse in Chicago was suddenly accosted one evening by two youths, one of whom was wielding a knife. The lady saw the youth approaching with the open knife pointed at her stomach. Her first reaction was to freeze, but then she remembered her authority as a child of God, and she spoke the Word. She said, "I plead the blood of Jesus against you, and I rebuke you in Jesus' name." Then lunging forward she said, "Give me that knife," and the youth released it into her hand. She then moved toward him and said, "You stand right there." Then she commanded the second young man—in the name of Jesus—to go into an adjacent building and telephone the police to come and pick the boys up. He immediately obeyed her. When the police arrived, the youth who had called them ran away. The police arrested the boy whom she had been detaining at knifepoint; later they picked up the other boy also. The lady was unharmed because Jesus said, *"Nothing shall by any means hurt you"* (Luke 10:19).

Just a woman? Yes, but she is *"mighty through God to the pulling down of strong holds"* (2 Corinthians 10:4). [11]

SPONTANEOUS OVERFLOWING

At the end of January, 1908, in Westport Hall, Kilsyth, Scotland, there was a visitation of the Holy Spirit that began spontaneously by the pleading of the blood. A brother named John Reid, sitting in the middle of the prayer group, suddenly raised his hand and started to plead the blood, saying, "Blood, blood, blood!" Immediately the Spirit descended upon the group, and thirteen young people went to their knees and began to speak in other tongues. It was the pleading of the blood that brought the outpouring.

It was around this same time that Mrs. Woodworth-Etter was holding her great meetings in Los Angeles and Chicago. She used to hold her arms aloft and say to the people, "I sprinkle the blood of Jesus upon you," and she made a motion with her hands as if she were actually doing it. People would come running to the front of the auditorium, and many fell prostrate, speaking in tongues and receiving healing.

The pleading of the blood was an accepted revelation of the Holy Spirit in the early days of the Pentecostal outpouring. However, like many other divine revelations, it was lost as man's organizations came in to replace the supernatural workings of the Spirit. Yet wherever this message is preached today, it is still received with gladness. And when the blood is used, it brings astounding results. Truly we are *"more than conquerors"* (Romans 8:37) through the blood (Revelation 12:11).

One of the early pioneers in Scotland, Pastor Andrew Murdoch of Kilsyth, received the baptism in the Spirit in early 1908. His wife received a vision of the blood running as a waterfall in her bedroom, and she was frightened. She cried out, "Blood, blood, blood!" and called for her husband. He assured her that this vision was of God. The same day she received the baptism in the Holy Spirit, speaking in other tongues. The Niagara of blood continued in her vision for a time, though, reminding her of the mighty stream that flows from Calvary, washing away sin and all uncleanness. The Holy Spirit gave these supernatural experiences to awaken God's people to the reality of the blood and its vital connection with the baptism in the Spirit.

OVERSIGHT AND OUTPOURING

In February 1908, a certain William Macrea was praying in his house in Kilsyth, and God made known to him by a revelation that two men were coming from Glasgow, intent on overseeing a church service. Neither of these men had received their Pentecostal experience. The Holy Spirit spoke and said that they were to be prevented from going to the platform. However, when the time for the meeting arrived, it was not easy to put this into effect, and the men were permitted to oversee the service.

Macrea kept the elders and deacons in a back room and asked them to plead the blood. While they did so, the Lord revealed all that was taking place in the meeting hall. One of the men from Glasgow got up to sing, but the Spirit revealed to the praying men that he was just showing off his voice! The elders and deacons continued to plead the blood, believing the Lord to work in the meeting. Within a few days, both men received the baptism in the Holy Spirit. In addition, forty-three were baptized in the Spirit that same weekend by the pleading of the blood. This is the way the outpouring of the Spirit began in Scotland in early 1908.

About this same time, several people journeyed from the United States to Kilsyth to receive the baptism. These people had been prayed for many times by the laying on of hands, but nothing had happened. But when they came to Scotland

and began to plead the blood, they all received quickly. No wonder John told us that the Spirit and the blood agree! (See 1 John 5:8.)

OVERCOMING UNHOLY INHERITANCES

I well remember the very first time I began asking for the Holy Spirit baptism in 1939. My mother and her family had been deeply involved in spiritism, which had affected our whole family. Many tragedies took place in our family because of this, although my mother was unaware of the cause. I suppose I was contaminated with this spiritism more than I realized, for spiritual filth spreads rapidly, and only the blood can cleanse it away. However, I was unaware of this contamination; I only knew that I needed the baptism in the Holy Spirit. I remember so clearly how I knelt down by a chair and began to pray. On and on I prayed, but never once did I plead the blood. I was in need of deliverance but did not know it.

Others were pleading the blood aloud, however, and suddenly I had a most amazing experience. A creeping rigidity took possession of my body, and I stiffened up and fell prostrate on my face as stiff as a rod. After a while, the stiffness left me, and I stood up, feeling quite embarrassed. An evil spirit had left me that I did not even know I had! No doubt it had entered me when I had experimented with table-turning as a boy of twelve, in the company of my aunts and uncles who thought it was a great parlor game. (Many think this of the Ouija board, but it is highly dangerous.)

A week later, I was even hungrier for the baptism in the Spirit and readily knelt down again. This time I started to plead the blood with enthusiasm. It was not long before I began to speak in tongues, and I have been doing so to this day.

PROTECTION FOR PASTORS AND THE HESITANT

I have prayed for many pastors and brought them deliverance, some in spectacular ways! Two pastors who came to us were saved from suicide and other spirits. Satan tries to discourage pastors, who are precious men in God's sight. If we can get one pastor delivered, we can get hundreds more delivered through their ministry! Pastors are tremendously open to temptations that do not assail their flocks. Pastors can fall easily into sin unless we pray for them. Never criticize a pastor; just pray with him and encourage him. Aquila and Priscilla did that with tremendous results for Apollos, who then became the leader of the New Testament apostolic church at Ephesus. (See Acts 18:24–28.) Pastors are growing hungry today.

God is making them hungry. God is moving by His Spirit with refreshing winds of new light and deliverance.

To the timid we would say, *"Have faith in God,...and nothing shall by any means hurt you"* (Mark 11:22; Luke 10:19)! If you enter in under the blood, you cannot be touched. You must be right with God. Every sin must be humbly confessed and put under the blood of Jesus. God is looking for men and women who will rise from the powerless mediocrity of our "churchianity" to the heights of sons and daughters of God, working with Him in the one New Testament church—His body, bone of His bone and flesh of His flesh. (See Genesis 2:23; Ephesians 5:29–30.)[12]

TRAVELING MERCIES

I have never known the active, audible pleading of the blood to fail. I travel much by car and much by air and have never failed to arrive at my destination on time to keep the Lord's engagement. I cover the car or the plane with the blood. As one blesses one's food by prayer, so we also protect our vehicles by pleading the blood.

I remember a brother in England years ago who, when faced with a car motor that would not start, just pleaded the blood because he knew nothing about automobiles. It started! When you find that difficulties are piling up against you or your family, just start pleading the blood and watch Satan's plans dissipate. It is surefire!

NO LIMIT TO USING THE BLOOD IN FAITH

In the early days of the outpouring of the Spirit in the twentieth century, Mrs. Nuzum of California used to teach her listeners in her Pentecostal meetings to sprinkle the blood upon their loved ones, their children, and all that God had given them. Didn't the children of Israel actually splash blood on their buildings? Is there any limit to using the blood in faith against satanic powers and the darkness of the world? Wouldn't it be good if congregations of Christians were to stand united in pleading the blood of Jesus against the demonic forces now trying to take over our cities and our young people?

I believe that the church has yet to discover the deeper dimension of spiritual warfare through pleading the blood. Great miracles can take place if we learn this secret. There is wonder-working power in the blood!

"There Is Power in the Blood"
(WORDS AND MUSIC BY LEWIS E. JONES, 1899)

Verse 1

Would you be free from the burden of sin?
There's power in the blood, power in the blood;
Would you over evil a victory win?
There's wonderful power in the blood.

Verse 2

Would you be free from your passion and pride?
There's power in the blood, power in the blood;
Come for a cleansing to Calvary's tide;
There's wonderful power in the blood.

Verse 3

Would you be whiter, much whiter than snow?
There's power in the blood, power in the blood;
Sin stains are lost in its life-giving flow.
There's wonderful power in the blood.

Verse 4

Would you do service for Jesus your King?
There's power in the blood, power in the blood;
Would you live daily His praises to sing?
There's wonderful power in the blood.

Refrain

There is power, power, wonder-working power
In the blood of the Lamb;
There is power, power, wonder-working power
In the precious blood of the Lamb.

twelve

The New Birth and the Blood[13]

I f there are degrees of intensity of miracles, and it seems there are, then the rebirth of a person's whole nature is the greatest miracle. The changing and cleansing of the human heart is an operation of spiritual surgery that would be impossible with the natural skill of man. As we shall see, Jesus the Great Physician takes the heart out, washes it, and puts it back an entirely new heart.

Jeremiah knew something of the essential wickedness of the human heart. He wrote, *"The heart is deceitful above all things, and desperately wicked: who can know it?"* (Jeremiah 17:9). *Young's Literal Translation* is interesting: *"Crooked [is] the heart above all things, and it [is] incurable—who doth know it?"* We see, therefore, that the very generator of our lives, that great pump of the heart, is a crooked, off-center thing; its nature is wickedness, and there is absolutely no natural cure for its state. It can only continue to pump pollution throughout the mind and body of man unless there is a radical operation.

Jesus left us in no doubt as to what this pump will do to us:

> *But those things which proceed out of the mouth come forth from the heart; and they defile the man. For out of the heart proceed evil thoughts, murders, adulteries, fornications, thefts, false witness, blasphemies: these are the things which defile a man.* (Matthew 15:18–20)

The mouth is the orifice through which the pump of the heart spews all kinds of filthy talk and behavior. Man cannot help it. He has been like that since Adam was kicked out of Eden. He is a fallen, pathetic creature. The driving power of our lives is the heart; and yet it continues to pump its garbage through our bloodstream. Is there any hope for us? We can understand what Paul had in mind when he wrote, *"O wretched man that I am! who shall deliver me from the body of this death?"* (Romans 7:24). Paul knew the answer: *"I thank God through Jesus Christ our Lord"* (v. 25). Jesus is the only answer; He must do the divine operation.

Unfortunately, so many wait so long before they apply for this radical operation. They try every means to ignore the impurity that is wrecking their marriages, their jobs, and their lives. They are indeed living in a body of death.

We have no chance; the heart goes on pumping, pumping, pumping death into our bloodstreams. We cannot get away from this death. We are trapped by a monster—Satan. As a male child is supposed to have its foreskin circumcised on the eighth day of its life, so we also are supposed to have our hearts circumcised as soon as possible. The younger the better, if we are to escape the dangerous actions of the heart.

SPIRITUAL HEART TRANSPLANT

Paul understood the mystery of this great operation. He expressed it in Colossians 2:10–12:

And ye are complete in him [Jesus],*...in whom also ye are circumcised with the circumcision made without hands, in putting off the body of the sins of the flesh by the circumcision of Christ...through the faith of the operation of God.*

In recent years, man has been able to transplant a human heart. This is an outstanding medical technique in which the arteries carrying the blood are severed, the diseased heart is cut right out, and the old muscle is removed and thrown away. In its place a healthy heart from a donor is quickly put into place. All the arteries are sutured, the clamps removed, and the blood allowed to flow again. This is the equivalent of changing a motor in an automobile. Some have lived for many years with a new heart.

To Bible students, this thought reminds us of David's cry, *"Create in me a clean heart, O God"* (Psalm 51:10). The Lord promised it to Israel and to all in New Testament Israel: *"A new heart also will I give you,...and I will take away the stony heart out of your flesh, and I will give you an heart of flesh"* (Ezekiel 36:26). This radical operation of

We must place our bodies on the altar as a living sacrifice.

God can be done only by His Son, Jesus. First, we must place our bodies on the altar as a living sacrifice (Romans 12:1). We must trust our whole lives to Him, knowing that He has the power to bring life out of death. We must be prepared to die, for obviously if

we receive a true circumcision (cutting round) of our heart, and then it is removed, the old man will die. This is what Paul meant when, writing to the Colossians, he said, *"For ye are dead, and your life is hid with Christ in God"* (Colossians 3:3).

Jesus takes the scalpel of the Word of God, which is sharper than any earthly instrument, and as we lie on the operating table of the altar of

God, He neatly inserts His knife, the sword of the Spirit, does a quick 360-degree turn, and all the vessels to our heart are severed. Then He takes our old sinful, dirty, crooked, wicked heart and cleanses it in the most concentrated disinfectant in the universe—the blood of Christ. In Joel 3:21, the Lord promises, *"For I will cleanse their blood that I have not cleansed."*

Once the blood has been applied by sprinkling from the hand of Jesus, our evil conscience is removed (Hebrews 10:22), and now our transformed heart is ready to be put back into our body again, for all the old filth and garbage has been destroyed.

I always remember my childhood in England when the garbage man would sprinkle carbolic powder into the bottom of our garbage containers, as a service from the city! It smelled

Jesus cleanses our dirty hearts with His blood.

very nice and destroyed effectively the corruption in the can. A dirty garbage can smells horrible, and so does a dirty heart, for the author of all corruption is Beelzebub, the lord of the flies from the manure pile. But the author of cleansing is Jesus, who sprinkles His blood on our dirty heart. Suddenly the heart is cleansed. It has been delivered from the body of death, for now a new heart is put back, miraculously sutured without a trace of surgery. The blood of our bodies becomes cleansed by this disinfectant, and now the body of death becomes the body of life. We are now walking *"in newness of life"* (Romans 6:4). We are those who *"are alive from the dead"* (v. 13). We died because our old heart was taken out. We live because a transformed one has been put back. This is God's great operation, and now the new heart pumps cleansed, life-giving blood through our body, which brings spiritual and physical health. The great miracle of the new birth is the basis of what makes divine health available.

MY CONVERSION

Within a very short time after I had this radical operation, my language changed. My mouth became filled with praise instead of swearing and off-color jokes. Any desire for liquor instantly disappeared, and my binding habit of tobacco smoking was miraculously broken when I prayed by myself in all simplicity. I suddenly felt the unclean habit, which was like a smothering sack, literally lifted off me. This was a miracle. My renewed heart no longer had any evil things to pump into my brain, and so a corresponding change naturally occurred in my body, which now obeyed my new heart. A complete transformation of character took place.

The first one to notice this change was my wife, and later she also found Jesus Christ as her Savior and the One who baptized her in the Holy Spirit; then she found herself a stranger in her church! No one ever spoke of the new birth in her staid denominational congregation. I was a member of another established church, but I had never heard anything about a radical surgical change in the heart.

Isn't it amazing that forms of religion can be developed around the old, unclean heart in the body of death? The very deceitful heart of man devises religious systems that put the worshippers into a spiritual torpor, so that they no longer are able to comprehend the way of salvation or their need of it. They attribute their weaknesses and mistakes to the weakness inherent in all mankind; this they describe as "human nature." They are right, but human nature can be changed to the divine nature. Peter knew it and wrote,

> *Whereby are given unto us exceeding great and precious promises: that by these ye might be partakers of the divine nature, having escaped the corruption that is in the world through lust.* (2 Peter 1:4)

To partake of this divine nature, we must have a cleansed heart and a new spirit; this spirit is the Spirit of Christ. Now, instead of our old heart pumping satanic filth, the renewed heart pumps the very nature of Jesus Christ through our veins because of His shed blood.

We are taught in the Bible a divine principle, that our life is in our bloodstream (Leviticus 17:11). This would seem to indicate that our blood carries the inherited sin of our forefathers. We cannot help being sinners. We are born with the corruption of Adam in our blood. We realize that such Bible teaching is totally abhorrent to those who go their own way, but how else are we to explain the continual appalling behavior of our fellowman?

Only Jesus can renew our sinful hearts.

Today crime in America has reached an all-time high, and police forces often feel that despite their best efforts, crime has taken over and is running amok. This is the only way that people in the United States and other "free" nations will be forced to cry to God for help, and His help can come only by Jesus performing the surgical operation of renewing the hearts of individuals. It is my prayer that God will change the hearts of our leaders. We are commanded to pray for them.

I exhort therefore, that, first of all, supplications, prayers, intercessions, and giving

of thanks, be made for all men; for kings,
and for all that are in authority....For this
is good...in the sight of God our Saviour;
who will have all men to be saved.
                                                    (1 Timothy 2:1–4)

If all the rulers of the free world were to have a true experience of the rebirth, it would transform nations within weeks.

In the Welsh Revival of 1904–06, crime largely disappeared. The police had nothing to do. The bars closed down; the theaters had no patrons. This can happen again, and I believe it is beginning to happen in this great charismatic restoration of the church.

MIRACULOUS RENEWAL

The renewal of the heart of the believer will be followed by the renewal of the body in health in this life, and then ultimately to a *"house not made with hands, eternal in the heavens"* (2 Corinthians 5:1)—an everlasting body! One miracle follows another. There is no limit to the number or quality of miracles that will daily occur in the life of one who has received the rebirth. In fact, as we have already shown, our very lives themselves become walking miracles. What a marvelous promise in these days of inflation and depression: *"But my God shall supply all your need according to his riches in glory by Christ Jesus"* (Philippians 4:19). There is no inflation or lack in heaven—just a steady flow of blessing, healing, and daily supply from an inexhaustible storehouse.

Jesus promised the same thing: *"But seek ye first the kingdom of God, and his righteousness; and all these things shall be added unto you"* (Matthew 6:33).

In the days that are ahead of us, before the great day of the return of Jesus, we are going to experience many amazing occurrences—special miracles and outstanding wonders that will confound the world. Our daily provision is in itself a daily miracle. Consider the Lord's Prayer when we pray, *"Give us this day our daily bread"* (Matthew 6:11). But this is contingent upon our being willing at all times to forgive those who trespass against us (v. 12)! As we seek to enjoy the Christian life to the full after our heart transformation, we enter into the life of continual miracles.

thirteen

Wonder-Working Power of the Blood[14]

In 1948 when the Lord began to open up my eyes to see the amazing authority that He has vested in us to work miracles, a particular promise of Jesus—*"Behold, I give unto you power* [Gr., *exousia*, authority]...*over all the power of the enemy: and nothing shall by any means hurt you"* (Luke 10:19)—became extremely dear to me. I was being used as a pioneer in what is now called "the deliverance ministry." I began casting out evil spirits from people who were cruelly bound by the enemy, and I saw tremendous miracles of physical and mental healing take place before my eyes. The first three were people with asthma, suicidal depression, and epilepsy. These three people are still healed today, over thirty years later. It works.

Having proved that we had the authority of Jesus to do these things, I suddenly realized that I was far out on a theological limb. No one understood. Other pastors in the city began to shun us, and I was no longer acceptable in the Toronto full gospel ministerial arena. To be alone—except for my wife, of course—and to be that far out on a limb seemed to be a dangerous position. This became especially obvious when Satan attacked my wife and me in the middle of the night by trying to stop our hearts from beating. We were cautioned to stop this ministry. I remember

In Jesus, nothing can harm us.

telling the Lord in prayer that if this amazing, miraculous ministry meant that I would lose my life, I was willing to die for His sake. From that time onwards, and by facing Satan squarely in Jesus' name and honoring Jesus' precious blood, I battled through to a deliverance ministry that I am told has influenced many men of God today to do the same.

What did Jesus say? *"Nothing shall by any means hurt you."* Nothing, absolutely nothing! No disease, no problem, no storm, no marriage problem, no financial disaster—nothing. Does this really apply to us? Yes, all of us. This covers anything that would bring hurt, harm, or injury and thus includes the whole area of accidents!

From 1948 to this year of 1979, I have found Jesus to be true to this promise. We speak the word of faith, coming from our hearts through the mouth, directed against Satan, and he gives way! He retreats; he runs before the blast from heaven that honors the name of Jesus, the blood of Jesus, and the Word of God, for we read a most simple statement of the early Christian martyrs: *"They overcame him* [Satan] *by the blood of the Lamb, and by the word of their testimony"* (Revelation 12:11). It was the living blood of Jesus—for His life is in His blood—and the Logos Word, Jesus Himself, spoken out of their mouths that drove back Satan and his demonic cohorts. Victory after victory occurred. Jesus is Victor, and so are we in Him. Your present life of defeat can change into a life of continual victories.

Those who overcame Satan in the early church were not always delivered from death or torture. They were promoted to a higher order of life through death, for it is written of them, *"And they overcame him* [Satan] *by the blood of the Lamb, and by the word of their testimony; and they loved not their lives unto the death"* (v. 11). Losing their lives here on earth was the means of gaining their lives in the next. If they had denied their Savior while facing persecution, they would have forfeited eternal life, for Jesus has said that if we deny Him in this life, He will deny us before the heavenly Father (Matthew 10:33). In our generation it is more likely that we will be delivered out of our troubles in this life if we are faced with persecution for our testimony. Either way, in life or death, we glorify God and maintain our victory in Christ. In Christ, there is no sting in death or life.

When Jesus said that nothing would hurt or harm us or bring us injury, He meant it. It is true, for He is truth.

SPONTANEOUS REMISSION OF DISEASES

Perhaps some of the most spectacular and exciting miracles are those that happen when people least expect them. People in the medical profession refer to these cases as "remissions," and, of course, though many of the medical doctors may not realize it, the Word of God teaches us that *"without shedding of blood is no remission"* (Hebrews 9:22). Because Jesus shed His blood for all mankind, it is possible for people to have a remission from their sickness or killing disease.

There is no question that in the Western world, many will pray for someone who is grievously sick. This is especially true among our churches. Prayer requests are sent in and congregational prayer is made, or the request is passed to intercessory groups and prayer chains that exist especially for this ministry. How can we understand the love of God when He brings a remission to someone who is not even aware that others far off and unknown have been praying for his healing? We cannot limit the hand of God in reaching down from heaven and "sending away" a sickness because Jesus shed His blood for all mankind. The expression "sending away" is the exact meaning of the word *remission* (Gr., *aphesis*).

THERE'S NO DISTANCE IN THE SPIRIT

I remember the time when the well-known missionary W. F. Burton of the Congo Evangelistic Band was dying of cancer in Congo. A lady in Melbourne, Australia, was awakened at 3 a.m. local time to pray for Rev. Burton, who was in dire need.

She obeyed the prompting of the Spirit and interceded for this missionary. At that exact moment of time, Willie Burton had a remission of his cancer. He later published photographs of the X-rays of his cancerous colon before and after this miracle. It was a spontaneous remission. It was a long time later that the truth was learned. From Melbourne to the Congo jungles is an extremely long way, but distance means nothing to God.

In our own church, we have often been amazed at the testimonies that have later been reported to us by people for whom we prayed in our regular services. We probably didn't even know them, but their case was reported to us, and usually before our opening time of prayer, we ask for congregational prayer requests. We do not do this as a formality, for experience has shown us that spontaneous remissions do take place in many cases. Of course, I do not even attempt to explain why some are not healed, but I suspect it may have something to do with the attitude toward God of the person being prayed for.

Not only are many sicknesses spontaneously healed, but it seems that a Spirit-filled Christian will automatically respond to another person's need. The Spirit in us seems to be most anxious to rise to the aid of the person who is stricken, and before we realize it, we are praying for that one. Many times when an airplane flies over, I find myself praying for the safe journey of those in the air. Is this a kind of superstition for the ignorant, or is it a God-given attribute? I think there is a connection here in Romans 8:26:

> *Likewise the Spirit also helpeth our infirmities: for we know not what we should pray for as we ought: but the Spirit itself maketh intercession for us with groanings which cannot be uttered.*

The *Amplified Bible* puts it this way:

> *So too the [Holy] Spirit comes to our aid and bears us up in our weakness; for we do not know what prayer to offer nor*

how to offer it worthily as we ought, but the Spirit Himself goes to meet our supplication and pleads in our behalf with unspeakable yearnings and groanings too deep for utterance.

The Living Bible translates it like this:

And in the same way—by our faith—the Holy Spirit helps us with our daily problems and in our praying. For we don't even know what we should pray for nor how to pray as we should, but the Holy Spirit prays for us with such feeling that it cannot be expressed in words.

Here we have a fact revealed. The Holy Spirit (not us) intercedes, prays, pleads, and goes to meet us in our desperate need. This is a spontaneous act of a loving God to start in motion a process to bring a miraculous remission to a person groaning in need. How wonderful that this ministry is inbuilt in the Spirit-filled church!

The Holy Spirit intercedes, prays, and pleads.

How do we know how many people may have prayed for one sufferer? How do we know how many people God may have urged to pray in distant lands? Suddenly a person is healed, and it is called a remission. Blood for blood. Jesus' pure, clean, precious blood for our sick, defiled blood. Remission.

THE MINISTRY OF KATHRYN KUHLMAN

The amazing ministry of Kathryn Kuhlman has proved this point beyond any further doubt. One of the leaders of the Catholic healing ministry, Father Francis McNutt, has explained that thousands of Catholics went to her meetings seeking healing and remission, and thousands of them found health. Miss Kuhlman's large healing services were in no sense a shrine. She happened to be a woman prophetess. She did not claim to be an evangelist or a preacher. She was certainly no healer—we leave that word to the metaphysicians—but she established a ministry where Jesus was honored through the omnipresent Holy Spirit, and people from all denominations came hoping or believing they would receive healing. Doctors were present to confirm these healings.

How do spontaneous remissions occur in such services (and they do!)? The answer must be found in the fact that the whole auditorium is charged with the presence of the Holy Spirit. The service is conducted in such a way as to cause people to expect the Holy Spirit to work. These healings are the sovereign work of God.

RECHARGING A DEAD BATTERY

If a dead battery comes in contact with a live battery, the energy in the fully charged cells goes into the dead cells. So it is in the case of the cells of the human body. The presence of disease means there are many sick cells, run-down cells, exhausted cells. They need a new charge of divine life. By entering an auditorium that has been prayed over, sung over, rejoiced over, and in which the blood of Jesus has been honored, the worn-out cells in weary bodies begin to experience a new charge of *zoe* life from God by the Holy Spirit. The presence of the Holy Spirit will send away, or remit, the sickness as a new infusion of divine life flows into the body. Remember that when God created man in His own image, He did so by breathing His divine breath into the lifeless form of Adam, who thereupon became a living soul (Genesis 2:7). The cells of Adam's perfectly formed body looked good, but they were dead cells. It took God's breath (Heb., *neshamah*) to bring full life and strength to Adam.

All of us are descended from Adam and Eve, and so when our cells are attacked by Satan with disease, there is a force far greater than the devil and sickness that can drive out disease, namely the very breath of God and the precious blood of Jesus, strongly present in these Kuhlman healing services.

THE SPIRIT AND THE BLOOD

If you put a damp, rotting object in a warm oven, the process of degeneration and decay temporarily ceases as the object is dried out. Where a sick person exposes himself to the warmth of the Holy Spirit, this "drying out" process begins to take place. After the decay has been arrested in the cells of the body, the restorative processes already resident in the bodily cells begin to take over, and with a supercharged "shot" of the Holy Spirit and life in the blood, healing may take place very quickly. This is a spontaneous remission.

Symbols of the Holy Spirit are fire, which cauterizes; water, which cleanses away dirt; breath, which revives and resuscitates; and oil, which soothes. All these represent the work of the Holy Spirit in a public meeting hall or church where Jesus is honored as Healer and His blood honored as a life restorer. Kathryn Kuhlman often said publicly that she could not understand why miracles took place in her meetings, for not all people who went had faith. Even if a person is compelled to go by a loving wife, husband, child, or friend, the fact that the person goes is in itself an indication of faith, however small. The fact that the loving relatives, who almost compel the sufferer to go, are all praying is reason for a miracle of spontaneous remission to take place. We are not always healed solely on our own faith. In fact, in deep distress and sickness it might be very difficult indeed for the sufferer to exercise faith at all. The fact that the person comes brings him or her into the power-charged presence of the Holy Spirit Himself, who intercedes for us.

Try to imagine a large healing service in which are many poor suffering people. Most of the people present are in an attitude of prayer, and this causes a spontaneous pleading by the Holy Spirit to the Father to release His life-giving breath to all. People in wheelchairs who have been unable to gain access into the main auditorium are healed in the outside passages, or even outside the building. It is sudden, it is spontaneous, it is a miracle, but it is Jesus who creates the remission.

As the church is increasingly restored by the Holy Spirit in the days in which we live, we shall see much more of this mass healing. In the Old Testament the priests were not able to stand to minister after the blood was offered, because the temple area was filled with a visible glory cloud.

Then the house was filled with a cloud, even the house of the LORD; so that the priests could not stand to minister by reason of the cloud: for the glory of the LORD had filled the house of God.
(2 Chronicles 5:13–14)

In Kathryn Kuhlman's meetings many people fell to the ground, either when touched by, or in the presence of, this lady. Many have queried this unusual manifestation, for admittedly it does not happen in many churches; but spontaneous remissions do not happen in many churches either, which is why people literally flocked to Miss Kuhlman's meetings to seek their healing. It seems that the falling to the ground may be a New Testament fulfillment of what happened in the Old Testament temple; the glory of God was present.

It is recorded in Luke 5:16–17 that Jesus withdrew into the wilderness to pray, and afterward He returned and started to teach doctors of the law who had gathered out of every town in Galilee, Judaea, and Jerusalem. In this unusual instruction class, *the power* [Gr., *dunamis*] *of the Lord was present to heal* (verse 17). The fact that Jesus Himself was there and that He was teaching the Word of God created a situation where any one of those learned doctors could have received a spontaneous miracle from the miracle-working power of the present Spirit.

When we have the same conditions today, we get the same results. When Spirit-filled men or women dare to get up and pronounce that Jesus is present to heal, the very air becomes charged with the healing virtue of God. It is not surprising that many who go into such a building do get healed.

Through the operation of several spiritual gifts, the Holy Spirit revealed to Kathryn Kuhlman with perfect accuracy the individuals who were being healed and the sicknesses from which they were receiving remissions, confirming the very real presence of the Spirit. This happened all over the auditorium, and then with the help of ushers, those healed were encouraged to come to the platform and testify. It was then that many fell to the ground under the power of God. Let it not be said they were *"slain of the Lord,"* for this expression is reserved for the enemies of God. (See Jeremiah 25:33 and Isaiah 66:16.) We sometimes get our expressions a bit mixed up! These coming into the strong presence of the Holy Spirit, who was honoring the evangelist, simply fell to the ground. They were not healed because they fell; they just fell! The priests in 2 Chronicles could not stand in the presence of the glory cloud—the *shekinah* of God. They were not slain!

LAST DAYS' EXCITEMENT

We can see the day coming when people will not only fall before the glory of God, but many may fall before they get into the church or public auditorium! In 2 Chronicles we read,

> *Now when Solomon had made an end of praying, the fire came down from heaven, and consumed the burnt offering and the sacrifices; and the glory of the LORD filled the house. And the priests could not enter into the house of the LORD, because the glory of the LORD had filled the LORD's house.* (2 Chronicles 7:1–2)

In the same way as many were healed just by being passed over by Peter's shadow (see Acts 5:15), so likewise many will be healed in the cities where divine healing services are held. Many sick people lying in hospitals and homes in these cities will suddenly come under the beneficent power of the Holy Spirit and will receive spontaneous remissions. The power of God will so greatly increase in the great restoration and renewal of the church that a saturation point will be created inside the church auditorium, and it will be so great that people will fall before the Lord in streets and on the steps of the building. The power of the Lord will be present to heal in a citywide sense.

These will be very exciting days. Keep in mind this Scripture: *"And a great multitude followed him, because they saw his miracles which he did on them that were diseased"* (John 6:2). Imagine what will happen in some of our modern cities when people actually fall down under the power of God and are spontaneously healed right on the sidewalks! Imagine the crowd of press reporters and TV cameramen who will quickly converge on such a scene, and afterward the publicity and the pictures, so that multitudes will see and believe on the Son of God. No wonder Kathryn Kuhlman was always saying, "I don't heal anybody"! These healings are from Jesus by the presence of the Holy Spirit saturating the auditorium. The only way to get our generation out of the impossible conditions of crime and debauchery that prevail is for signs and miracles to take place on a large scale. Then people will follow Jesus, not politicians!

If only the church in past generations had worked true miracles by the power of the Holy Spirit and by honoring the blood of Jesus, Satan would have had much greater difficulty in getting his show on the road. A large section of the Christian church has denied the power of God and not expected any miracles and has taught people that the day of miracles has passed. While they are saying this, the day of miracles is rapidly reappearing for them to see.

Some Bible colleges and schools actually forbid their students to speak in tongues, to pray for the sick, or to cast out demons, and yet they advertise themselves as Bible colleges! When Jesus walks in their doors in miracle form, through any member of their student body, they reject him or her, thereby rejecting Jesus. It is time for the whole church to be shaken from top to bottom by a return of miracle-working men and women in our midst. The whole creation groans and waits for the manifestation of mature, miracle-working ministers of God. This is the time that a great maturing is taking place. It is the time of the outpouring of the latter rain. It is now.

End Notes

1. This excerpt, which begins on page 26 with the heading "Deliverance to Life," is taken from *Demons and Deliverance*.

2. This excerpt, which begins on page 34 with the heading "God's Equations," is taken from *How to Receive the Baptism in the Holy Spirit*.

3. This excerpt, which begins on page 43 with the heading "Speaking Out," is taken from *Demons and Deliverance*.

4. This excerpt, which begins on page 57 with the heading "Covering Our Children," is taken from *Demons and Deliverance*.

5. This excerpt, which begins on page 74 with the heading "A Spirit of Suicide," is taken from *Demons and Deliverance*.

6. This excerpt, which begins on page 92 with the heading "Our Value in Him," is taken from *Pulling Down Strongholds*.

7. This excerpt, which begins on page 106 with the heading "The Blood and the Word Gifts," is taken from *Charismatic Gifts*.

8. Chapter 8, "The Blood and Divine Health," is comprised of excerpts from *Divine Health*.

9. This excerpt, which begins on page 127 with the heading "Continual Cleansing from Spiritual Poison," is taken from *Is Mark 16 True?*

10. Chapter 10, "Holy Spirit Baptism and the Blood," is comprised of excerpts from *Bible Baptisms* and *How to Receive the Baptism in the Holy Spirit*.

11. This excerpt, which begins on page 152 with the heading "Protection from Muggers," is taken from *The Working of Miracles*.

12. This excerpt, which begins on page 157 with the heading "Protection for Pastors and the Hesitant," is taken from *Return to the Pattern*.

13. Chapter 12, "The New Birth and the Blood" is comprised of excerpts from *The Working of Miracles*.

14. Chapter 13, "Wonder-Working Power of the Blood" is comprised of excerpts from *The Working of Miracles*.

about the author

H. A. Maxwell Whyte

The picture of a British bulldog, H. A. Maxwell Whyte (1908–1988) had a commanding countenance and a stentorian voice, which was especially awesome when raised against the devil and his demons. He had a big, soft heart, and he loved Jesus. He was a pioneer in this generation in recognizing that *"we wrestle not against flesh and blood, but against principalities, against powers, against the rulers of the darkness of this world, against spiritual wickedness in high places"* (Ephesians 6:12), and he carried the battle right to the enemy's doorstep. He had faith enough to believe that God would confirm His *"word with signs following"* (Mark 16:20). In the powerful name of Jesus, he proclaimed liberty to the captives and opened the prisons for those who were bound (Isaiah 61:1). For more than forty years, he ministered worldwide to the downcast and brokenhearted and led the way in the ministry of the powerful gifts of the Holy Spirit.

Maxwell Whyte was born on May 3, 1908 in London, England. As a child he was raised in a

nominally Christian home in which church attendance was encouraged. Raised as a Presbyterian, Maxwell was strongly influenced by the godly pastor of his boyhood parish, and at age sixteen, he made a commitment to the Lord, although his level of understanding of what this decision meant was meager indeed.

After completing his education at Dulwich College in London, Maxwell entered the business world as a representative of the Anglo-American Oil Company, and even during the depression years, he enjoyed a measure of success that was the envy of many during those years of economic stress. On June 8, 1934, Maxwell married Olive Hughes in St. Paul's Anglican Church in the London suburb of Beckenham. It was in this peaceful residential area that Maxwell and Olive rejoiced in their comfortable lifestyle, their solid marriage, and the birth of their first two sons, David and Michael.

All was going well for this successful and happy couple until son David became seriously ill. In fear that their son might be taken from them, Olive and Maxwell cried out to the Lord in desperation, and they were both dramatically affected when God restored David to good health. Shortly after this experience, Maxwell was invited by a colleague to attend a small charismatic meeting in Croydon on the outskirts of London. There, for the first time, he witnessed the operation of the gifts of the Holy Spirit and saw a group of people whose relationship with the Lord was one of vitality not in keeping with religious tradition. Maxwell's life was never the same again as he was truly converted, baptized in water, baptized in the Holy Spirit, and miraculously set free from a smoking habit, all within a few weeks. The year was 1939, and to be a charismatic in those days was not a popular place for a Christian to be!

At the outbreak of World War II, Maxwell entered the Royal Air Force as a signals officer, where his lifelong interest in amateur radio was put to use in setting up defense communications. During his six-and-a-half years of military service, Maxwell spent many long hours studying the Bible, convinced that one day he would enter into full-time ministry. In 1946, after his discharge from the RAF, Maxwell returned to his business career only to leave it a few months later to prepare for the ministry. After several months of intensive training and prayer, Maxwell answered the call to emigrate to Toronto, Canada, to be pastor of the United Apostolic Faith Church, a small congregation that had been without a pastor for several years.

So it was in April of 1947 that Maxwell and Olive Whyte and their family of three boys (Stephen was born a few months after the war) arrived

in Canada to take up the responsibility of leading a group of a dozen or so believers who made
up the fledgling congregation in Toronto. The
first few years in Toronto were not easy for the
Whytes. They lived in cramped quarters on little
income, and in 1952 a fourth son, John, was born.
The boys adjusted well to their new environment
and soon became full-fledged Canadians. For
over three decades, Maxwell faithfully served as
pastor to this church. He witnessed the transformation of the small band of worshippers as God
built them into a thriving group of believers who
held to the charismatic truths of the Bible.

In 1948, while Maxwell was dealing with one
of his parishioners who suffered from chronic
asthma and another who was suicidal, God sov-
ereignly directed him into an understanding of
the reality of spiritual warfare and deliverance.
This revelation catapulted Maxwell into a ministry that drew attention from many parts of the
globe.

In over forty years of ministry, Maxwell ministered in many countries of the world on five con-
tinents. At the same time, he authored at least
eighteen books dealing with the workings of God
in the present charismatic outpourings of the
Spirit. Hundreds of letters have told of the healings and deliverances of those who have read his
writings, believed, and been blessed.